THE SHARECROPPERS COMMUNITY

White Gold "Cotton" Part II

Charles Watkins III

Library of Congress Control Number: 2020924713

HARDBACK: 978-1-953791-74-0
PAPERBACK: 978-1-953791-73-3
EBOOK: 978-1-953791-75-7

Ordering Information:

For orders and inquiries, please contact:
1-888-404-1388
www.goldtouchpress.com
book.orders@goldtouchpress.com

Printed in the United States of America

TABLE OF CONTENTS

DEDICATIONS

Two very special people, made it possible for me to achieve many of the life goals. I am eternally grateful to both of them.

This book would not have been possible, without the tutoring, I received from Dr. Joan Campbell. A student at Jackson State University.

Dr. Joan Campbell, encouraged to read, express myself, helping me find the passion of writing. My personal experiences, regardless of whether the experiences were encouraging or discouraging. Committing ideas on paper, in way that entertaining. She, told me, to find my own writing style, run with it.

Thank you, Dr. Campbell.

The second individual helped me with a several aspects of my life, including putting me on a path to meet Dr. Campbell. This talented, dedicated man, Roy Curry. During High School, assured me that attending College, was within my reach. I had no idea he had grown up in Clarksdale, Mississippi, knew the sharecroppers' struggle first-hand.

Coach Curry, believed sports provided a structure opportunity, to develop the skills, needed for success in our society. Thank you, the time devotion, developing my football skills. Earn all-city recognition, lead to my education at Jackson State University, to all good things that have come since.

Thank you, Coach Curry.

Charles Watkins III

EXPOSITORY WRITING

Expository writing is a type of writing that is used to explain, describe, give information or inform.

Expository writing is different from other forms of writing, such as fiction and poems. Most expository essays, have an introductory paragraph, in which a thesis, objective is stated. several main body paragraphs that prove or explain what is in the introduction and a concluding paragraph in which everything is summed up.

ABOUT THE AUTHOR

Born in West Point, Mississippi, move to Chicago at the age of (2) years of age, moved back to West Point, Mississippi. I worked, lived with the on the outskirt of Clay County, near West Point, Mississippi. James Thomas Brand, the Landowner Plantation. My education was built around the cultivation, the harvest of the "WHITE GOLD COTTON" called cotton. Worked as a full capacity worked in the cotton field. Chopping cotton, plowing the mules picking cotton all of the manual labor that made the farm successful and productive. On a plantation area called "MUDA", a short word, for the Bermuda land, for it beautiful grass. Working on that rural farm, with my grandparent for (8) years. Southern High School law was established. Children that lived with their grandparents, from the north, were not from the state of Mississippi. The unadopted Children, no longer l attend school in Mississippi. My (2) two brothers and I were taking back to Chicago to live with our parents once again.

The inspiration for creative writing, that drive me to take people on the private journey. My gestures to expressive feeling, the readers, painting of my visual view daily activities. Personal feeling, I would like the reading audience to experience, vision the journey, from Chicago to Mississippi as a child. The (12) twelve hours, which expected of the field worker on the plantations. I was motivated to navigated travel the journey of "The Sharecropper Life", personally as a child. Most Sharecroppers, were unable to verbally, articulate their feeling openly, while living on the plantation. I've been blessed by God, place many people in my life that have guided me. Dr. Joann Campbell, her tutoring, me for (3) three years. The

English composition at Jackson State University. Dr. Campbell took a Sharecropper Grandson, taught me the fundamental of writing. Sharecroppers Grandparents Son, that had worked countless hours as a labor, on a Plantation Farm. far less than in a classroom.

WHITE GOLD "COTTON" The Sharecroppers Stories, will give you the inside feeling the Sharecroppers trials and tribulations in their daily life. My adolescent years in 1960's years in the habitation with my grandparents. The Sharecroppers Stories, touches their strong spiritual faith in the almighty "God", the power in the word of "God", how God always made a way under any circumstance. Faith was the key nutrition that kept them going, 1865 through 1970s which was the start to the end of the majorities of Sharecroppers due to the fact of modern technology "The Cotton Pickers"

INTRODUCTION

This is my story about working on a plantation in Rural Clay, County, Mississippi, when I was a boy. My grandparents, Charles and Alice Watkins Sr., were Sharecroppers. I worked alongside them daily from the ages of 7 to 15.

Sharecropping, was a hard life, my experiences give you a sense of just how hard it was. The book's title is a long-used characterization of Cotton, reflecting its important role in the economies of the South, the United States, other areas around the world.

I started this book so I could pass something on to my children, to teach them, more about me, our family.

Although I was born in Clay County, my parents took me to Chicago when I was 2 – I don't remember anything about those first two years, of course -- and back to Mississippi when I was 7. Eight hard years later my parents took my brothers and me back to Chicago. Moving from the big city to the deep rural South was an enormous change for a 7-year-old; moving back to the big city after those eight years was another huge change.

The experience of living with my grandparents, has never left me. While it was a shock to find myself living a hard life, I learned, a lot about myself, about people – city people, country folk alike.

"GOD'S LOVE FOR ME, BACK TO YOU."

CHAPTER 1

THE NORTHERN MIGRATION

The Great Migration, the relocation of more than six million African-Americans from the Rural South, to the Northern Midwest, from 1916 to 1970. This was a significant impact, on many of the nation's urban areas, where African Americans, had started to, over populating, the north metropolitan area

Driven from their homes, by unsatisfactory economic opportunities, harsh segregationist laws, many African Americans, headed north to find jobs as, industrial workers. The job opportunities developed during World War I. As industry geared up to supply the allies, again later during World War II. There were increasing opportunities, for African American, to migration to the northern states.

The great migration from ,1910 to 1930, added significantly to the populations to, Chicago, Detroit, Pittsburgh, New York, Washington, D.C., and other cities.

The draw was economic: the prospect of better jobs, for skilled and semi-skilled workers, promised to lift many out of poverty. Unfortunately, moving north led to many encounters, with racism, poverty and tension in their new communities.

As people migrated from the South's, rural areas to the cities, the number of black-owned businesses increased, to serve those African Americans, now living in the cities. (Jim Crowe Law, white-owned businesses wouldn't serve them).

Migrating to the north from the south, would increase their wages from, $2.00 or $3.00 dollars, for a 12 hours day, of work, to a significant amount, $20.00 or $30.00, working the same 12 hours, a day work. For those who found jobs, they could make as much in one day, as they did in a month as a sharecropper.

There also were great opportunities, for African Americans, to do well in many other ways, as their newfound purchasing power, enabled them to provide comfortable lives, for their families. Comfortable living, most only dream of as a sharecropper. African American, now could educate their children, purchase a house, and purchase a business. The most significant prize would be, send their children to college, to become teachers, doctors, lawyers, business people, whatever they wanted to become.

Some African Americans had problems adjusting, to their improved financial situation, the temptations of a big city. Some had no self-control, didn't invested their time wisely,

Unfortunately, some of the country males, abusive to their families, treating them the same way, they had been treated by the white landowners back home. The better standard of living, and opportunities for women to find work, the family dynamics were very different up north. Some African Americans, males and females, could not adapt, would leave their families without continuing to support them.

The African Americans families, without a bread winner, would become especially vulnerable, as the mothers often were unable to support their children.

This was one of the worst results of the big migration. Fathers in the South seldom left their families.

Of course, many African Americans, men did very well in providing, everything necessary for their families. Some men took the opportunity, to educate their children, sustain, improve the standard of living for future generations.

My parents left Mississippi, for Chicago, when I was two years old, to find a better way of life. The Sharecroppers in Mississippi, finding better work, a higher standard of living up north, was an easy choice. My mother joined my father in, Chicago after he had been there one year. As boy, recall my father did well, providing food and clothing. He also had was interested in, the importance of getting an education.

Living Chicago, with my mother after my parents had separated, recognized the challenges in providing for the basic needs for five children, my life was getting ready to take on a drastic change for the worst. Back in the 1960s, the laws didn't place as many requirements, fathers to support their family.

I could hear the adults talking about the trip to, Mississippi, nothing was clear just small conversations, among the adults in the family.

As we preparing to leave Chicago, my cousin, speculated that once we reached Mississippi, the next step, would be would become a cowboy. We had many relaxing days, just watching televisions. We also would act out, that we were some of those popular cowboys on television. My vision of Mississippi, was The Wild, Wild, Old West!

We arrived in West Point, Mississippi, late in the summer of 1957, after driving all night. We were packed in that car as if we were just going to church. We were unaware, that ride would be 11hours long. During the long drive, the car's suspension groan from its heavy load: Grandma, two brothers, two sisters and I, with my father driving. For 11 hours, we were packed in that car like sardines in a can.

During that car, ride the early morning sunrise, gave me an entire new outlook thing were going on outside of Chicago. Upon our arrival, when we saw the rural area. where my grandparents lived, their ugly house, this was horrified feeling that I never experienced. We never imagined; we would spend the next eight years there.

Our grandpa's reception, was not very friendly, either. He must have known, that we had no idea, the involvement living on a plantation, in rural Mississippi. Now, we would be his responsibility, to teach us.

When our father indicated, we were going to Mississippi, we thought this would be a family vacation! Instead, my father stayed only for one day, then drove back to Chicago. My father youngest brother went back to Chicago with him. John was his name.

My father took John, back with him to Chicago, leaving my sisters, the three boys, like we were hostage's exchange. They were leaving the children to work the farm, taking my uncle, to a better life in Chicago. We were unaware, how long we were supposed to live with our grandparents. We were unaware, the time point for my father return.

No one asked us, of course.

Our ages: Ella Bell 8; Samuel, 5; Daniel, 4; Peggy, 3; and Charles 7.

The most refreshing observation, was the Mississippi, fresh air. Oh, how refreshing my lung felt, similar to the scent of water, where fish are dwelling. The water affects the air, in ways that please your lungs! Upon my arrival to Mississippi, there were several smells that were unaware. The other country smells, that aren't very pleasant, such as manure. The cow manure was everywhere, from the cow eating grass.

The fresh air, open field, trees, those different smells and observations were the highlight of our arrival. While living in Chicago, unaware of the things, that nature had to offer. The beauty of been able to walk around with asking your parents, amazed of the outdoor beauty free-spirited. Chicago, boy raised in a totally different environment, now in Mississippi, a different world now.

Prior to leaving Chicago, things had changed, there were a great deal of uncertainties, a feeling of being displayed. I anticipated, meeting my grandma mother, at that time, waited on the opportunity to go to Mississippi, "Down South," that was the common words, that was a spoking among the adult, from the south. We were never giving detail or plans. The only explanation, we are going to the south, where the cowboy lived the Wild, Wild, West to visit. The <u>Cowboys,</u> I would love watching on television, (Example; Roy Roger, Gene Autry, and the other Glamorous Cowboys. I couldn't wait to get dressed in my cowboy outfits, on my arrival to Mississippi. This was my vision of going down south to visit my grandparents. One of the most exciting things, to meet my grandparents, for the first time. I had been told by my father; his mother would be coming to meet me. My father mother, would be the person that would be taking us to Mississippi, to spend time with her in the south, during our vacation. I wanted to pictures how my grandma would look; I was very visual, from looking at television. Chicago, highly restricted from going outside of the house, without supervision. Any time we wanted to go out of the house, we had to have permission. Mostly of our activities inside of that apartment we couldn't go outside of the apartment. Elvis Presley, on the television, was one of my favorites, the way he talks, the way he moves, not judging a person by his color. Curiosity ran wild in my mind about my grandma appearance, what would my grandma look like.

From my observation from television, my visual of my grandma, was the lady on the pancake box, at that time. The lady Aunt Jemima, a southern African American, lady that was picture her resemble. Upon my grandma and father arrival, she a kind looking lady, looked overjoyed to see us, with open arm, wanting to know something about us. I was my mother's boy, had giving my mother a tremendous challenge, just raising me as a son. I was a very curious child, like most of Chicago, children were at that time. As a child in Chicago, everything that we participated were inside, of the building. My favorite time in which could experience, the outdoor, walking to school. Going home from school, in my opinion, was so joyful, enjoying the outdoor. Walking home from school, open a whole new world, step in puddles of water. Prior to going to school every day a reminder, stay out of the water. It's guaranteed, if there were any puddles of water anywhere, my feet would be wet on my arrival home.

(wet shoe and wet feet.)

As a child, going outside, to the local Park and the Riverview Carnival. My sister Ella, love the outdoors, she persuaded me, to ride on a rollercoaster. Riding on the rollercoaster, this everything like the Six Flags Amusement Parks. The entire experiences, felt like we were was in an airplane 30,000 feet, in sky, getting ready to fall, from the sky. My sister Ella, she was outgoing, fear nothing, joy from riding the roller coaster.

On that day, my grandma and father arrived, to pick us up, we had a joy of excitement of anticipation. We were leaving, that night going to West Point, Mississippi. The 12 hours trip from Chicago to West Point Mississippi, would be an experiencedly, like the Roller Coaster ride at the Riverview Amusement Park. Everybody was packed into that vehicle, that would ultimately take us to my grandparents' home. At that time during my journey, remember how fast; those cars were around our own car. My grandma and father appeared to talking in some type of code, we could not understand. This was not the first time, hearing my parent's talking in those codes. Highway 57 South, two ways, lanes Highway, indication you had an oncoming driver drive that was coming toward you going the same highway. The cars passing each other, just by a few inches. Only seeing bright head lights, once they appear to get closer, to the oncoming car, both my father while drive would change the bright light, to a lower light. Numerous times, the car wouldn't change from their bright lights, to their lower beam light, as a curiosity oncoming driver wouldn't change these bright lights to lower lights than my father would turn his bright light back to bright. Shortly after that occurred it appear that both drivers agreed with each to other about the use of their lights. This was tremendously exciting taking this ride out of Chicago on the road, couldn't recall at any time taking a trip out of Chicago.

CHAPTER 2

THE PLANTATION OLD HOUSE

Grey is the best color to describe how our grandparents' house looked. It probably was white at one time, over the years, all the paint had peeled off. The wood on the house didn't have any sign of a color.

The house was very old. It sat on 3'x 2' blocks, you could see clearly under the house, from front to back. During the summer, it was cool under there, sometimes Samuel, Daniel and I, would play marbles, under that old house.

The house had a peaked roof, with rust in some places, time had made a serious statement. The roof had a gable on one side. There also was a porch in front of the main entrance, with two large windows facing the front of the porch and three supporting columns around the front of the porch. The roof also extended over the porch.

It was designed in two sections, with the gable of the roof, indicating where the rooms were separated, from one another. Three rooms faced east, three faced wests. Although it was dilapidated by this time, you could tell the house was designed well. Many years earlier, it could have been the home of the plantation owner or overseer of the property.

The six rooms, were used for living purposes; two were used for storage. The family slept in two other rooms. Inside, the main hallway separated the rooms.

There was a pantry on the back porch, where fresh homemade canned goods were stored, curing smoked meat, curing salted meat, always pork meat never beef. The meat hung from the unfinished pantry ceiling so pests couldn't get to it. In the morning, often there would be fat back pork, bacon, or fat back meat fried hard and crispy.

The kitchen had a look of its own, though it was not particularly large. There was a wood stove with an oven for baking. Loading the stove with wood was the first order of business, with getting the fire started second. The firewood was stacked against the back wall. My grandma used that old stove to cook a lot of things, most often fried fish or chicken, corn bread and pork fat back meat.

Toward the center of the kitchen, there was a table used to make biscuits, cut meat, and cleaning wild games. Underneath the table there often was a slab of heavily salted meat fat back meat that was used for cooking and seasoning, including turnip greens, mustard greens, and collard greens. This salty fat back meat had been part Southern African American, diet for generations.

We used the entryway to keep our boots, coats, and any other items such as watermelons that my grandfather sold in the summer. The watermelons, were kept the hallway to prevent anyone from stealing them. Occasionally, while unloading the watermelon, we would drop one – by accident, of course - so we could enjoy fresh watermelon, too; otherwise, our tight-fisted grandfather would sell it all. Sometimes there would be as many as 30 watermelons in the hallway.

Finally, there was a large living area where we spent most of our time. The room's focal point, a large fireplace, provided plenty of heat, when we need it. In that room, we did homework, talked, rested, and cooked snacks (peanuts and sweet potatoes) on the fireplace.

Too make those snacks, we would dig a hole in the ashes, place the sweet potatoes in it then cover it up for about 15 minutes. Uncover the potatoes, wipe them off with a wet towel and enjoy! To make the fresh roasted peanuts, we'd place them on the brick in front of the fireplace.

Its take three minutes cover the peanuts with ashes, after about three minutes, beautifully roasted peanuts.

The fireplace had large hearth, providing enough space to prevent hot ashes, fire to get on the floor. Back then people didn't have fireplace screens.

In that large room, we had two big beds along with some small chairs around the fireplace. There also was a small black-and-white television set.

My grandma had a great assortment of handmade quilts that were thrown across each bed for additional warmth. During the winter, the sheets were made from cotton seed sacks, which were just the right size to cover the bed. The sheet would always go between the quilts, keeping us toasty warm.

The Firewood used were cut with an axe, by hand. We kept a large supply of Firewood stacked up outside; Firewood for the fireplace was about 2' long while Firewood for the stove was about 10" long.

We would have a large stack of Firewood available, wood was used for cooking and heating the house. A big black pot that held several gallons of water. A fire under the pot would boil the water, so my grandma, could wash our clothes, especially white garments. In addition, she would use the pot to make lye soaps, for bathing and another household purpose

Wooden latches on the wall held the door, in place once it was closed – that was all the security we had, most days. When we were away, from the house for a long period of time, my grandpa used a large chain with a padlock to secure the door.

On the kitchen side of the house, there was a fenced-in area for our livestock – you could see them from our kitchen window. There also was a walkway to a nearby, levee where people would take their cattle to graze. We also fed our hogs food scraps; they would eat anything.

On the other side of the house, we had a chicken coop. It smelled pretty bad. The chickens slept in the coop, laid their eggs each morning.

Our grandmother, also had clotheslines, in the yard, for drying clothes after they'd been washed. Where we lived, washing machines were rare and dryers unknown.

Outside the house, not far from the kitchen, was a public water pump. None of the houses on the plantation had inside plumbing to provide running water. This was the only source of water for the entire community.

The water pump was at least 20 yards, from our house. The old pump had a large handle, you would have to pump at least 10 times, before seeing any water come out. The pump handle was hard work, it always squeaked.

Gathering around the well was popular, neighbors could catch up with each other, with small conversation.

Most families, would store some water at home, too. Grandma had a 50-gallon barrel to collect rainwater, which we would use to wash clothing and for drinking.

Running water isn't the only thing you don't have without indoor plumbing: you also don't have bathrooms. For that purpose, we had an outhouse.

An outhouse is a small building, a short distance from the residence, containing a toilet. The small wooden building provided privacy, protection from the elements. Most of the outhouse were square or rectangular. Although, Thomas Jefferson, designed, built octagon-shaped outhouses, at one of his homes.

The outhouse usually was located some distance away from the house, and from any fresh-water well, to minimize the risk of contamination and disease. There was no connection to a sewer or septic system, there was no sewer or septic system.

Toilet paper wasn't always available or affordable, often one would find old newspapers, catalogs from Sears, Roebuck, Montgomery Ward, which doubled as reading material. The paper usually was kept in a container to protect it from mice.

CHAPTER 3

SHARECROPPERS SCHOOL

We arrived in Mississippi, just in time for the new school year.

Ella and I, were of school age, so we needed to get started for classes.

We were surprised to learn there was only one school. Abbott School, it only had one room! The school served students in grades 1 through 12. The teacher knew most of the families, including mine.

Until that time, I had never even heard of a one-room schoolhouse although over the years, learned they were common in Rural areas. The South Naturally, was a big different than the Chicago, education system. I knew first-hand from Chicago, expected that every school had many rooms.

On the first day of school, the teacher asked Ella, what grade we were in. My sister indicated, both of us were in the second grade. Fortunately, for me, the teacher knew different.

As the youngest, they put me in first grade.

The other students, enjoyed hearing our "funny" northern accents. Most of the students as well as the teachers enjoyed having conversation with us. What were so amazing about those students, they had an accent, that were very interesting as well. The south students, had a vast knowledge, pertaining to how to be successful in the south. We were in for challenges That didn't' make it easier for us.

My Grandparents lived, in a community called, "The Muda." that lived on this small Plantation, that had great rich soil for growing cotton and soil beans. This community was made up, with 13 Families, in this area sometimes, referred to as the Quarter. Most the people had very little formal education with books. However, they could grow their own food, repair their cars, cut each other hair and respected their neighbor. The Muda, was a helpful community, the people shared with each other, looked for each other children. The neighbor would keep an eye out for others child most time. (If you done something wrong, if a neighbor saw you, they would inform you, don't make me tell your parents.) We didn't have any telephone. The mobile cell phone, wasn't invented at that time. School was challenging for all the children who lived in the Muda. Education was the lowest priority to Sharecroppers; most children would not finish school due to this factor. Sharecropper children often fell behind in their studies, parents (or grandparents) would rather have them working on the farm, rather than being in a school.

Likewise, our grandpa, would allow our grandma to take that responsibility, he kept his opinion to himself. However, our grandma would not allow us to miss school. To her, school was more important than just about anything else we could be doing.

The school based its schedule on the cotton harvest however, all the children would be helping on the farm in whatever way they could. Once class started again, our grandma made sure we were back at our little desks.

* * *

Teachers and ministers in the plantation areas were admired, they were among the bright lights in the community.

In each of the nearby communities, it seemed there were a couple of families with a long line of teachers, they were highly respected. It was passed down from generation to generation with a great deal of pride.

* * *

Most sharecroppers were pessimistic about education. Our grandpa was pretty typical in this regard in, that his primary concern in life, was to have a good cotton harvest. Our grandpa what step feed his family, having a great Harvest, would enable him to provide for the family. He didn't see how formal education played any role in a successful harvest.

This attitude was easy for the adult sharecroppers to embrace, their own education was so limited.

The educated, African American, in our area were ministers, teachers, some landowners whose parents had instilled strong educational values, in them since childhood. My mother's sister, Aunt Janie Bell, (For example, had two girls and a boy. Aunt Janie insisted her children, take education Seriously, recognize their own value.)

Education, in most situation, create well value in their home, the local community.

Aunt Janie, was the head cafeteria supervisor at Beasley, a rural public school. Her husband L.T. Walker, lived on their own property. Each of the children eventually, had their own homes on that location.

After college, Ella Lee, returned to West Point, Mississippi, to be a social worker, going door to door to teach sharecroppers ladies, pride in themselves, to value their home and family. All of her children also attended college, she was a leader in her community.

Mossy Walker, was Ella, youngest sister became a teacher, after finishing College at Alcorn University. After teaching in West Point, Mississippi, for a while, she would take her teaching skills to live in Minnesota. One of her children played football, for the University of Minnesota, later played for the Chicago Bears. Aunt Janie's family, was proud of the two girls attending college, always showed guests their college yearbooks. Their brother, L.T. Walker Jr., stayed in West Point, Mississippi, worked on the farm and Bryan Brothers Packing Co. The family took great pride in the estate, that had been in their family for nearly a century.

Mostly all in rural Clay County were Sharecroppers, they didn't act the same, shared certain characteristics. (For example, those who were uneducated had broken spirit,) not much in the way of dreams of a better future. The Sharecroppers, weren't aware of the new mechanical cotton pickers, that within a few years, would reduce manual labor substantially.

West Point, Mississippi, was the Clay County seat. African Americans, who lived in town, had lifestyles completely different from the Sharecroppers. The city-dwellers, worked in a wide range of capacities, including teachers, meatpackers, steel workers, housekeepers, and several owned funeral homes, barber shops, beauty shops, auto repair shops, farms and other businesses that served other African Americans -- who were not welcome at white-owned businesses.

In the city, many African Americans, were established, just as well as, the white residents. African Americans Doctors, were especially respected. My Uncle Cal, on my mother's brother, married a African Americans Doctor's, daughter, her father lived in one of the largest homes in West Point, Mississippi. My Uncle Cal, worked at Bryan Brother Packing Company. Bryan packing Co., was one of the most economical advantage, contributors to West Point, Mississippi, African Americans.

My grandma, she took proud in us going to school, getting educated for some reason. She knew more than we, give her credit about knowing, what could happen in the future. Nevertheless, my grandma didn't want us to pursuit the future uneducated. My observation, some of the children on the "Muda", didn't attend school at all. The parents of those, children hadn't finish elementary school, High School, graduate view as something very special. The parents, wouldn't invest time money for basic educational values. The people in that "Muda", community's people, had enough education to take of their needs, for that area. The people mostly, didn't have much, you could almost live off the land, they had their own way of communicating. The "Muda", was the end of the road, the "Muda", had their own dialect.

My grandpa, shown his dialect as well, my grandma, for some reason, look toward the future, in us through education fundamental in reading, writing, and arts. We spend a great deal of time as children, trying to figure out, my infatuation of art and craft, as a boy on the Muda. Living in the rural part of the south, work was manually, with their hands, passed down for generations.

CHAPTER 4

PLANTATIONS AND SHARECROPPING

Mild winter, hot summers, provided perfect conditions for growing cotton. As a result, beginning in the 1600s, farms, then plantations sprung up, throughout the South, to produce the "WHITE GOLD COTTON."

The Plantations, ranged from 500 to 1,000 acres, with each acre capable of growing about 5,000 plants. The plantation owners, recognized that using slaves would keep costs down. Even though slaves were expected to work up to 18 hours a day. Most plantation owners, did not feed them well, treat them well or provide decent housing.

By 1860, southern plantations supplied 75 percent, of the world's cotton, were shipments from Houston, New Orleans, Charleston, Mobile, Savannah, and other ports. The insatiable European, demand for cotton fueled by the industrial revolution, which created the machinery factories to process raw cotton into clothing. The raw cotton was cheaper to make handmade products. European and New England purchases soared from 720,000 bales in 1830 to 2.85 million bales in 1850, to nearly 5 million bales in 1860. Cotton accounted for 60 percent of American exports. [1] [2] [3]

With so much land, the plantations were large enterprises, in many ways, self-sufficient, with the main house, slave quarters, a dairy, blacksmith, laundry, smokehouse and barns. The plantation owners hired overseers, to manage the operations of the slaves. The overseers faced pressure to maximize profits, which they would do anyway they could.

Slaves often lived in basic crude, wooden cabins, consisting of one or two rooms with dirt floors. The owner, meanwhile, lived in Georgian-style mansions, with ornate columns and large verandas.

With the abolition of slavery, the end of the Civil War, its lingering effects, the cotton plantation economic model faced significant challenges, Sharecropping was the answer.

Sharecropping is a form of peonage: debt slavery or debt servitude, in which an employer compels the worker to repay debts with work. Although Congress outlawed peonage in 1867; with Reconstruction southern African Americans, were swept into this form of peonage, that lasted well into the 1940s. "WHAT IS SHARECROPPING"? The employers, would advance workers, cash or goods. The Sharecroppers workers, agreed to go without further cash payments to repay the debts at the end of the cotton harvest. The Sharecropper, use what little money they had, for living expenses.

The Sharecropper had little chance of repaying the debt, they would work without cash payment for long stretches.

This arrangement was not limited to cotton production, African Americans, were where common in many poorer regions of the United States. Tennessee Ernie Ford sang in his hit song, "Sixteen Tons," the coal miner would "owe my soul to the company store." [4][5] encounters, with encounters, with encounters, with encounters, working to only pay for food, housing and supplies.

Sharecropping is a system, of agriculture which a landowner allows a tenant to use the land, in return for a share of the crops produced on their portion of the land. The southern economy in disarray, after the abolition of slavery, the devastation of the Civil War. The White, landowners wanted to reconstitute a labor force, as quickly as possible, while freed African Americans, wanted autonomy, economic independence.

Many former slaves expected, the federal government to give them a certain amount of land as compensation, for work they had done as slaves. Union General William T. Sherman, had encouraged this expectation, in early 1865, by granting a number of freed men, 40 acres each, of the abandoned land left in the wake of his army. [6]

During the final months of the Civil War, tens of thousands of freed slaves, left their plantations to follow General Sherman's victorious army, across Georgia and the Carolinas. In January 1865, in an effort to address source of the growing number of refugees, Sherman issued Special Field Order Number 15, a temporary plan granting each freed family 40 acres of land on the Georgia coast. The army also donated some of its mules, no longer need to carry war materiel, to the former slaves. [6]

The "40 acres and a mule" policy gave hope that the freedmen, would be able to work their own land, after years of servitude. Owning land was recognized as the key to economic independence.

Unfortunately, as one of the first acts of Reconstruction in 1865, President Andrew Johnson, ordered all land that was taken into federal control, be returned to its previous owners. The Freedmen's Bureau, established by Congress, to aid the millions of former slaves after the war, had the sad task of informing freed men and women, that they could either sign labor contracts, with the planters or be evicted from the land they had occupied. Those who refused or resisted were eventually forced out by army troops. [7]

The former slave owners were determined to re-establish a gang-labor system similar to the one used slavery. Supporting this effort, in 1865 and 1866 legislatures in the former confederate states passed restrictive "black codes" legislation denying blacks legal equality and political rights, and requiring them to sign annual labor contracts. [8] [9]

The inability to buy, own property left the former slave's, little choice but to work on their former owners' plantation on the owners' terms. As a result, freedom meant exchanging slavery for sharecropping – and perpetuating poverty for generations.

In exchange for the use of the land, a cabin and supplies, landowners divided the plantations into plots, of 10 to 50 acres, for farming by each family. The sharecropper would grow the crops, give a portion of the proceeds, usually half, to the landowner. The landowner also would extend credit, to the sharecroppers to buy goods, from their dry goods stores. The charge for the interest rate would be as high as 70 percent a year. [8] [9]

A Republican victory, in the Congressional elections of 1866, led to passage of the Reconstruction Act of 1867, revising aspects of the initial program. The Act was concurrent with passage of the, 14th and 15th amendments, which granted blacks the right to vote, equality before the law and other rights of citizenship.

This freed the former slaves, from the hated gang-labor system, giving them autonomy as they went about their daily business. However, it often resulted in sharecroppers – black and white - owing more to the landowners for the use of tools and supplies. (For example, then they were able to repay, some Blacks managed, to acquire enough money to move from Sharecropping, to renting, owning land, towards the end of the 1860's. Many went into debt , were forced by poverty on the threat of violence, to sign unfair and exploitive sharecropping, labor contracts, that left them little hope to improving their situations.

Not all whites who lived in the south were land owners, some migrated to the poorest parts of Mississippi, were able to purchase farms, so the less fortunate white families signed on as tenant farmers or sharecroppers, too.

A man named Luther R. Mills, was one of the first sharecroppers. He became a sharecropper on January 1, 1866, about nine months after the Civil War ended.

Two Mississippi soldiers, who had served the confederacy met with a Union officer one day in late 1865. One of the former rebels, was L.P. Thomas, a landowner who wanted to ensure his cotton was harvested, the other was Mills, " African American, which he lately owned." No longer a slave, Mills wanted to provide for his wife and three young children.

Thomas and Mills had written a contract on a form provided by the Freedmen Bureau. In it, Thomas agreed to provide the Mills family "free of charge" with clothing, food, living quarters, medical attention when needed, a garden, and humane treatment. In exchange, Mills agreed to work for Thomas for the next year. Mills signed with the contact with an X as he could not read or write.

Mills agreed to work for his former master, he could not find work anywhere, couldn't buy a farm himself. Even 50 years later, neither Mills, nor any of his descendants were able to own their own farms – 90 percent of African-Americans were either sharecroppers or tenant farmers still. Progress was slow: in 1960, nearly 80 percent of southern blacks still worked as sharecroppers on land owned by white people.

Sharecroppers, seldom made improvements to the farms, which they did not own, often the landlords often to let the property fall into disrepair, since they did not live there. With so much of the crop.

going to the landowner. The Sharecroppers, there was little incentive to work as hard as the business of farming required.

*   *   *

In my grandparents' area, there were about ten families who lived in an area called the Quarter, and sometimes the Muda (short for Bermuda grass). My grandparents lived on a subset of the Muda.

Owned by James Thomas Brand, the" Muda was an old plantation homestead manor covering more than 500 acres. The African Americans, had worked the land for more than a century. Brand was one of the largest landowners in that area – the "Muda", was just one of the farms he owned.

Indeed, Brand owned the entire district, even a part along the highway that he named Brand Town. He located his cotton gin in Brand Town, where his family also lived. When I was down there, he employed hundreds of African Americans, families as sharecroppers.

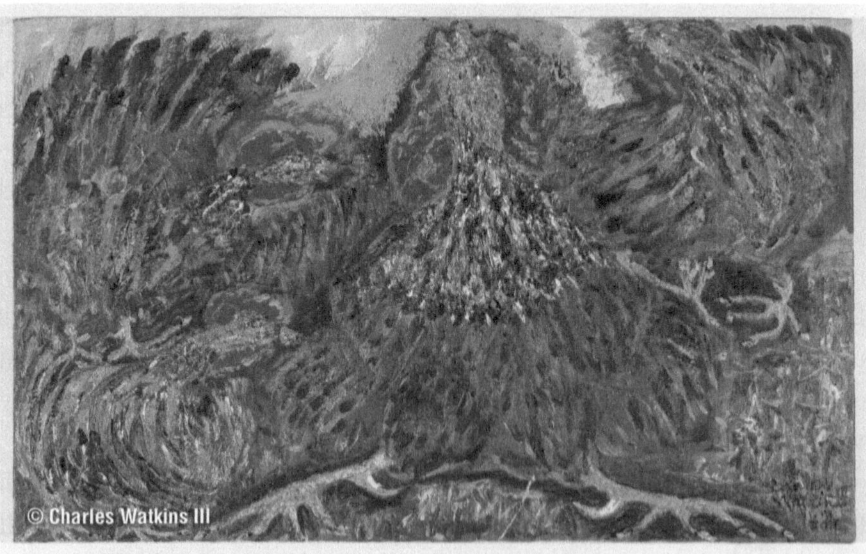

A POEM BY, CHARLES WATKINS III

THE LITTLE RED ROOSTER

This morning, my little red rooster crow,
for day light.
This morning, cock-a-doodle-doo,
its 5 a.m.
I have not heard him crowing, for daylight…

Where is my rooster? Where could he be?

I know he is the best rooster, I've ever had, in the "Muda" barn yard.

Maybe, he heard me sing that, Sam Cooke, song. "If you see my little red rooster send him home".

It's 5 a.m.

Like a clock, he crows.

My father said, "nothing is like a good red rooster."

The hen house is so happy. Where could he be?

Little red rooster crowing, for daylight.

That my alarm clock, to start my daily activities.

That red rooster is, my alarm clock.

I need to hear from him, yes to start, my day.

Where could my little red rooster be? – Where could he possibly be hiding? Why is he not crowing for daylight?

This is a clever rooster; maybe he found another hen house.

Hey, hey, hey, I'm looking for my little red rooster, If you see my little red rooster, please send him home.

If see my little red rooster. Yes, singing that Sam Cooke song, 'if you see my little red rooster'

Please send him home; I need a rooster for my barnyard.

CHAPTER 5

"COTTON"

WHITE GOLD "COTTON", is a long-used characterization of cotton, reflecting the important role it has played, continues to play in the United States, in world economies. The Cotton bits, pieces of cloth have been found in Mexico, dating from as long as 7,000 years ago. In the Indus River Valley in Pakistan, cotton was being grown, spun and woven into cloth nearly 5,000 years ago. The Indus River Valley, (5,000 years ago) around that time, natives of Egypt's Nile River Valley, were making, wearing cotton clothing." [10]

"Arab merchants, brought cotton cloth to Europe about 800 A.D. When Columbus discovered America in 1492, he found cotton growing in the Bahamas Islands. By 1500, cotton was known generally throughout the world. Cotton seeds, are believed to have been planted in Florida in 1556, in Virginia in 1607. By 1616, the Virginia, colonists were growing cotton along the James River." [10] Cotton production, took off after the Cotton Gin, became widely used in the early 1800s. The Cotton

Gin, made it possible to supply large quantities of Cotton fiber, to the textile industry all around the world. The Cotton fabric accounts, for half of the fiber worn. It is a comfortable choice, for a warm climate, it absorbs moisture well. In the United States alone, the U.S. Cotton Production rose from 73 bales, in 1800, to 2,136 bales in 1860, to 10,266 bales in 1900. [11]

The major use of cotton today is for textiles: clothing, towels, bed sheets and many other products. Other important products, of the Cotton plant include, cottonseed oil, for salad oil, snack food, cosmetics, soap, candles, detergents, paint; The hulls and meal are used for animal feed; other byproducts include cellulose, fertilizer, fuel, tire cord, pressed paper and cardboard.

"The growing season requires 160 frost-free days, which means Cotton is grown, between the latitudes of 45 degrees north ,30 degrees south. The major producing countries are the United States, People's Republic of China, India, Pakistan and Uzbekistan. It also is grown in Argentina, Australia, Brazil, Egypt, Greece, Syria and Turkey. Today there are five prominent types of cotton grown in the world: Egyptian, Sea Island, American Pima, Asiatic and Upland." [12][13]

Cotton plants are perennials, almost always grown as annuals. Growing annuals, rotation the crop each year, helps prevent, minimize disease, over the long growing season. The Cotton plants, begin to appear, within a few days of planting; Pretty yellow flowers, appear about 45 days, after planting. As the flower withers and dies, a seed pod – called a boll -- forms. When the boll matures, it breaks open, exposing fluffy cotton. In some areas, the plants grow 5' tall.

Gossipier hirsute (the scientific name for Cotton) accounts for approximately 90 percent of today's, cotton production. Each plant has a main stem giving rise to several branches at the top. The leaves of the plant are arranged in a spiral on the branches, have long petals and three to five triangular lobes. The plant produces a single flower on each branch that can be red, purple, yellow or white. It forms a leathery, oval seed capsule or ball that is 1" to 2" long. Mature balls usually open to reveal the white cotton fibers and seeds. The cotton plant can grow as high as 5' and is usually cultivated at the end of the growing season.

Cotton is a shrubby plant, that is a member, of the mallow family. Its name refers to the cream-colored fluffy material, surrounding small cotton seeds, called a ball. The small sticky seeds must be separated from the wool to process the cotton for spinning. weaving. Deseeding cotton, is cleaned, carded, spun, woven into a fabric, that also is known as cotton. Cotton, is easily spun into yarn, twisted naturally, interlocked for spinning.

America's Cotton Belt, runs east and west, including parts of California, Alabama, Arkansas, Georgia, Arizona, Louisiana, Mississippi, Missouri, New Mexico, North Carolina, Oklahoma, South Carolina, Tennessee, and Texas. United States cotton farms produce about 16 million bales a year, third only to India's 27 million bales and China's 21 million bales. [14] Cotton is the United States', most valuable agricultural product. [15]

PEST THAT ENDANGER THE COTTON PLANTS

It's not easy being a cotton plant.

The boll weevil (*Anthonomus grandees*) is cotton's best-known nemesis. The weevil, is a type of beetle, that feeds on the buds, flowers in the Cotton bowl. More than, 100 years ago, the boll weevil migrated, into the United States from Mexico, spread rapidly. Over the years, the pesky insect, has cost U.S. Cotton producers more than $15 billion, in lost crops, costs to combat it. In the late 1950s, the U.S. Department of Agriculture, created the Boll Weevil Research Lab, which quickly went to work, to combat the weevil's destruction, prevent its spread to other states. Although the industry remains vigilant, the boll weevil is not much of a problem any more. Indeed, the National Cotton Council, declares boll weevil eradication, as one of the greatest advancements of the U.S. cotton industry. [16]

Bollard Cotton, is the trademark given to a number of varieties of cotton bio engineered by Monsanto Co., to resist the weevil. Commercially available since 1996, Bollard Cotton accounts, for more than one-third of all cotton grown, in the United States. This product has reduced, the use of insecticides, the associated production costs. [17]

In addition to the Boll Weevil, other insects, weeds and grasses also pose problems for Cotton plants, by sapping the moisture and nutrients in the ground. Bermuda grass (*cynodont diction*) long has been a problem for cotton plants. Grown as a turf grass or as forage for livestock, the hardy Bermuda grass, also can act as an invasive weed. It was introduced from Africa (not Bermuda) in 1751, spread rapidly throughout the southern, southwestern states. It often is planted for beautiful, durable lawns; nutritious and traffic-tolerant pastures; golf courses; athletic fields and more. The perennial grass grows best in tropical, subtropical and transition zones. [18] Many homeowners like Bermuda grass for their lawns because it can withstand hot weather and weeds.

As you'll read in the next chapter, cotton farmers spent a lot of time keeping weeds at bay by "chopping" the cotton.

Cotton is ready to harvest, about four months after planting. When the bolls split open to reveal the white cotton fibers.

Once the plants mature, fields are usually picked every three to four weeks to prevent the fibers from attacked by pests. The entire field is usually harvested within or three or four pickings.

THE COTTON GIN

The development, perfection of the cotton gin, transformed Cotton, from a big business to a huge business. Its fundamental operation, is to separate the fiber, from the seeds. The Cotton Gin, vacuums raw cotton into tubes, that carry it to a dryer to reduce moisture, improve the fiber quality. It then runs the cotton, through cleaning equipment to remove leaf ash, sticks, other foreign matter.

Samuel Slater, an English mill worker, migrated to America in 1790, built (from memory) the first cotton mill, in this country. [19][20] With Slater's construction of a mill, Eli Whitney, saw the opportunity to develop a faster way, to remove the lint from the cotton bolls. He produced his first Cotton Gin, with partner Phineas Miller, obtained a patent in 1794. [19][20]

The Cotton Gin's, potential was immediately apparent: It could process, more cotton in an hour, than several men could process by hand in an entire day. Patent law, at that time being relatively new, poorly enforced, the two partners' patent didn't stop others from pirating their technology. [19][20]

Whitney's, machine made it possible to produce 50 pounds, of cotton lint daily. Cotton, became the South's leading cash crop, more profitable than tobacco. Slogans, including "cotton king" and "king cotton" were popular during these boom years. The American south, was supplying 75 percent of the world's Cotton supplies, by the time Civil War, broke out. [19][20] The wealthiest landowners, of course, were in the best position to profit from processing, selling cotton, often with their own Cotton Gin.

THINGS TO KNOW ABOUT COTTON

Can you eat cotton seeds? The best answer is no, you should not eat cotton seeds. Cotton plants produce a natural chemical called gossypol. In humans, gossypol affects the heart, liver. The reproductive tract, abomasum's kidneys also are affected. Monogastric, animals such as horses, also are susceptible to gossypol poisoning. While the ruminants, such as cattle and sheep, can tolerate higher levels of gossypol. Eventually, though, gossypol exposure can be toxic to cattle over enough time. Common symptoms to gossypol exposure, include weakness, loss of appetite, depression, difficulty breathing, blood in the urine, inflammation of the intestine and reproductive problems. No cure exists. Extracting the cotton seed, from the animal will reverse the effect, is not certain to eliminate it. Some animals have died within two weeks of the seeds' removal. [23]

There are several species, of wild cotton that grows around, the world but is not cultivated. These species are found in Africa, Arizona, Australia, Brazil, California, Central America, Mexico and some tropical areas. Cotton species, are difficult to refine, they aren't harvested. [22]

Like many agricultural crops, Cotton, has benefited, from genetic assistance and breeding. In the United States, Cotton growing stretches, from California to Virginia, covering more than 14 million acres (about 22,000 square miles). [24]

CHAPTER 6

CHOPPING COTTON AND
PICKING COTTON

Working in cotton fields was hard work. Working in these fields often meant 12-hour days or longer (sunup to sundown) during the peak summer months.

Despite the tough physical labor, Sharecroppers, pride in their work provided a structural, discipline, helped them get through those, long days, perform their work efficiently. If the work wasn't done correctly, you had to do it over, learned at an early age, it wouldn't get finished. The workers (my grandpa, for example) would not be satisfied if the job wasn't done correctly.

Most of the Cotton growing season, centered on two tasks: chopping cotton to reduce weeds so the cotton plants could grow, picking cotton for the harvest. Not just simple manual labor, chopping and picking cotton required skill and dedication. That's why it's a thing of art.

CHOPPING COTTON

Chopping cotton, was the process of thinning out, the cotton plants, using a hoe, so that the best plants have the best chance of developing into mature plants. Cutting an occasional plant in each row give the remaining plants, more space to grow. In addition, weeds would be removed with the hoe to keep them from crowding the cotton plants. On the farm, there were some herbicides used, nothing as sophisticated as those today.

All Sharecroppers, performed these tasks, learning using the same fundamental technique, been proven to be the most effective and dependable. The Sharecropper took pride in their work.

Obviously, the Sharecroppers, were the most important persons, in cultivating the crop. Many Sharecroppers, used mules to help them, and the mules were essential to productivity.

Mules resulted from breeding horses and donkeys. Compared with horses, mules had more endurance, more resistance to disease, stronger hooves, needed less feed and were less likely to be spooked. Mules often are mistaken as stubborn, that's not the case. Mules inherit intelligence from the donkey and speed from the horse. [26]

Chopping cotton, though, was strictly the Sharecroppers' work, as it required hands not hooves. The Cotton choppers used both eyes and hands to determine where to chop, with the hoe, much like looking ahead while picking cotton. You would go to the next boll of cotton, to pick the cotton, picked while filling the left hand (or the lead hand) with the excess cotton to put in the cotton sack. Mastering the hand-eye coordination, for chopping and picking were hand-eye coordination. This were the same for playing a musical instrument, required for hitting a ball with a bat, or using a computer.

PICKING COTTON

Picking cotton by hand, enables the farmer to pick the cotton without disrupting immature cotton bolls, that were still developing. In addition, the farmer knew all the cotton plants were picked clean.

It should be no surprise the term cotton picking originated in the southern United States, where it usually is pronounced "cotton picking'," in the late 1700s. It differs from the 19th century Dixie term "cotton picker" in that the latter term was considered derogatory and racist. [28] "Cotton picking" referred directly to the difficulty and harshness of gathering the crop while "cotton picker" alluded to the tough, calloused (and usually black) hands that picked cotton.

Mechanical cotton pickers started appearing on some plantations and it was a long way from being perfected. Of course, farmers who picked cotton by hand were happy to point out the mechanical picker's shortcomings, including:

- The mechanical picker was so heavy the fields had to be dry.
- The mechanical picker would damage plants still growing, costing the farmer money by reducing the yield.
- The mechanical picker was expensive to buy and expensive to operate, unlike the hand pickers.
- Before the picker could be used, all the leaves had to be removed from the plants because the picker grabbed everything in its reach.[30]

Over time, though, the mechanical picker was improved to the point that it became a valuable tool for cotton farmers.

In 1936, the Rust Cotton Picking Machine was demonstrated at the Delta Experimental Station near Leland, Miss. Though the device was not yet perfected, it picked cotton well enough to cause a sensation, provoking fears mechanical picking would destroy the sharecropping system during a time when millions already were out of work. [31][32]

Deere & Co. of Moline, Ill., had experimented with stripper type harvesters and variations of the spindle idea, but abandoned them in 1931, finally resuming development of a picking machine in 1944, after buying several patents. Deere began production in 1950 of two-row pickers that could harvest twice as much as the one-row machines common at that time. [31][32]

Cotton growers embraced mechanization long before other southern farmers. The writing was on the wall, accelerating the rural migration to northern cities.

The two predominant ways cotton is harvested in the United States today involve mechanical cotton pickers or cotton strippers.

A cotton picker, used mostly in the southeastern, mid-south and southwestern states, pulls the lint from the plants while bracket holds the plant to avoid damaging the rest of the plant. In the High Plains of Texas, cotton strippers are prevalent. The stripper takes more of each plant, requiring additional processing at the cotton gin and more frequent cleaning of the stripped

When my brothers and I were in Mississippi, however, our grandparents' farm was too small to have a picker so our jobs were secure, at least.

Picking cotton required using hands and eyes in a rhythm. This was so important because the first bolls to open were at the bottom of the cotton plant. The hands would have to move in a way that it wouldn't damage the cotton bolls that had not yet matured. The immature cotton would open in time for the second or even third harvesting.

Hand picking was taught at an early age so that youngsters could develop their skills. Naturally, some people were better at chopping cotton, and some were better at picking cotton. (My grandfather was better at chopping cotton, for example.)

Picking cotton started in September and continued through Thanksgiving, by which time 98 percent of the cotton would be harvested.

When we started our days picking, the overnight dew covered everything, especially the big cotton plants with freshly open cotton to be picked. If you weren't careful, your clothes would get soaking wet in no time. To stay dry as possible, we would use the big cotton sack as a shield as we walked to the end of the cotton row.

Cotton sacks came in different sizes, from 4' tall for children to as long as 6' for adults. Each person would pick cotton until the sack was full; then you'd weigh it so you could keep track of how much had been picked. Some people wore knee pads to avoid hurting their backs.

Most of the time, you would start picking at the back of the rows, move toward the front, so you would have a full sack, by the time you reached the scale. We would pack the cotton tight in the sack to carry as much as possible.

Each time your cotton sack was full, you would carry it to the cotton house for weighing and tallying. The tally was a reckoning, score or amount to keep track of the cotton. You would stay at it until your sack of cotton weighed 75 or 85 pounds, a goal you'd try to reach before lunchtime. In the most situations, an adult would pick 250 to 300 pounds a day. If the head of the household could set that amount, the rest of the family would contribute to picking up to 1,200 pounds, which could then be taken to the Cotton Gin. The 1,200 pounds of raw cotton, would typically yield about 650 pounds after the seeds, leaves and such were removed in the processing.

Whenever you picked, you would see Cotton Bolls, that weren't yet open, know you would be back for them. By the end of the harvest, you may have been through the field four times to get all the Cotton.

In November and December, people would use the expression "pulling the cotton" to describe how you could pull the boll and all into the cotton sack instead of picking the cotton out of each boll. This was a faster way to get the last of the cotton out of the field. The compensation was lower ($2.00 per 100 pounds instead of $3.00per 100 pounds) at that time of year, however, the cotton was of lower quality. Cotton pulling was a form of stripping, that made it more efficient to pick cotton at the lower price.

During the chopping cotton phase, people were paid from sunup to sundown, which during the summer months meant many, many hours. With the picking taking place during the shorter fall days, getting paid by the pound was better for the landowners. (Some pickers were known as "400 pounders", they could pick 400 pounds in a day.)

The Sharecropper, worked nearly all year, harvested most of the cotton before receiving any cash payment for the harvest. This end-of-year profit sharing, was called the settling-up day. When the landowner would tell the Sharecropper about the proceeds, profit for the year. Settle-Up, this was the time, when the land owner would, go over all the expenses for the year harvest. The Sharecroppers, would receive, what money was left over once the land owner, deducted all the expense.

Most Sharecroppers, considered the art of picking cotton by hand, one that could be put to use in everyday life. (For example, they would grow a variety of vegetables, fruit for their own nutrition and survival, including green beans, potatoes, berries, plums, peaches, nuts, corn, strawberries, butter beans and watermelons.)

In fact, picking cotton was less difficult than some of the other crops, such as butter beans. With butter beans, you had to example the pods by hand to see whether they were full or just looked like it. If the butter bean pod felt full, then it was ready.

Mainly, Butter Beans, were so close to the ground, this was back-breaking work. Butter Bean pickers, also were paid by the pound. Just as with cotton, you would pick all day and keep track by the weight.

Picking Strawberries, also was hard on the back. Breaking the stem about a half-inch from the berry, enabled it to roll into the palm of your hand. Using both hands, you could get three or four berries. You then carefully place them into your container, repeating the process until the container was full. These, too, were bought by the pound.

CHAPTER 7

THE SHARECROPPERS FAMILIES

Despite the brutality of slavery, there was gender equality among the African Americans men and women. The plantation system, was based on" PATRIARCHY", a social system, in which males, generally hold the primary power, leadership, moral authority, social privilege, control of property. This patriarchal model, transitioned to the sharecropping, had opportunity if the land owner treated the Sharecroppers fairly.

After emancipation, most former slaves sought to re-establish their families, bringing back with those family members, who had been sold to other plantations. At the same time, the focus of the Sharecroppers' Labor switch to serve the needs of the household, rather than the landowners.

Hard physical labor, was the key to supporting the family. Most families in the south, were led by fathers, as the bread winner, mothers as the homemakers. Both parents, usually with less than a high school education, would bring balance to the home, providing a source of security, for the children and grandchildren.

In almost every family, there was a strong woman, who worked with her husband to earn a living off the landowners' land. The African American women, had major plans in the education of their children for the future. (In many cases, the wives would be more educated, could read and count better than the husbands.) Women were stalwarts of their families and communities – as they are today.

*   *   *

Our grandparents, had inherited five young grandchildren, with the expectation that they would provide shelter, food, care for as long as we were on the Muda. When we arrived, Ella Bell, 8; Samuel, 5; Daniel, 4; Peggy, 3; Charles, 7.

Our grandmother opened her heart to us, taking on the role of our mother. We could count on her, to be there for us whenever needed. She took us to school activities, allowed us to visit our mother's relatives, as often as we want.

My sister, Ella, was very talkative, more so than the other girls her age, in our new school. She was smart, as well, often able to figure out a lot merely by observing. There plenty going on around us, all the time. As the oldest, she was stronger than the rest of us, could outrun, outjump any boy her age. Ella, assumed the responsibility of being our leader. This was especially true at school, where she often fights my battles for me.

I had something inside of me it's going to be just find, mostly affected by the drastic changes in our lifestyle and environment.

Our grandma, had raised three boys, she took Ella, with her everywhere, never leaving her by herself. Grandma, knew of rural males, who had taken advantage of young girls, if were left alone. My grandma, was not going to let anything happen to her granddaughter.

Ella and I, were old enough to be expected, to help out around the farm. We had to help out around the house, doing chores, working in the cotton fields.

We were just old enough to be effective, the move from Chicago to Mississippi, our other sibling, Samuel and Daniel, must be feeling with all the changes, in our lives as well. When I look back at situation, how they were coping with, our new life reality myself, overwhelmed, worry about only, how *was going survive this living situation.*

We called Peggy, the youngest, Baba, a nickname our mother gave her. (My mother had nicknamed me June Bug. That name stayed with me until, the age of 13, then my name changed to junior)

Shortly, after 3 months, our mother came to Mississippi to take Peggy, back to Chicago. home. Her arrival was a complete surprise to us, our mother was a beautiful, elegant lady. While she was there, she took us to stay with her and her mother and Mr. Shaffer. For two weeks, it was just like old times, she cooked, washed clothes, helped her mother in the kitchen.

Once the two weeks ended, she took us back to our father's parents', house so she could say good bye again. It wasn't until then that we learned Peggy, was the only one going home, our hopes again crushed.

At the same time, I didn't want to leave our grandmother, who had worked so hard, given us so much love, to feel at home with her. I felt a strong bond with her, enjoyed the sense of security, in her love for me. In this regard, I felt fortunate that it wasn't up to me where I lived: I'd hate to tell my mother or my grandmother that I chose not to live with either of them. That would have broken their hearts as well as mine.

It was obvious my grandparents, had worked hard over the previous two weeks, cleaning up and fixing up their old house. It looked a lot better than it had before.

Yes, finally we were going back to Chicago, though nothing was said about it, the rest of us wanted to think, we would get to go home soon as possible.

A few months later, our mother returned to get Ella. By this time, I'd seen enough of rural Mississippi. I always, wanted the best for my sisters, the best place for girls to grow up, was Chicago. I was relieved that she could go back to Chicago. As before, I figured it wouldn't be long, before the boys would be, going back home, too.

Samuel and Daniel, my two brothers had their own ideas, about what was happening around us. We weren't old enough to discuss it, complain about our grandparents, every day was shocking to me. We knew that we were better off, most of the Sharecroppers children, on the Muda.

* * *

Our mother had grown up in large family with a strong father, Jordan Johnson, and mother, Ella Johnson. With their 13 children, the Johnsons farmed 50 acres, supported themselves well. My mother, Flossie, had sisters Janie, Bell, Bessie, Minnie, Emma, Edna and Pauline; brothers Jordan Jr., Albert, Henry, Cal, Pirl and Sam, the youngest, very outgoing a leader of the family

(Sadly, grandpa Johnson passed away in 1945 and Ella later married J. Hugh Shaffer, a man who owned his own farmland. All his family, lived on this estate, which included a large pond (with fish!) and dairy cows. Mr. Shaffer, was a World War II veteran, he maintained a military bearing. From everything I could tell, he was a smart man.

(He always had modern, farm equipment to cultivate, maintain his property. The large lawn on the property always looked well kept, as did the dairy farm and fields. I was told that many white people respected the WWII veterans, Mr. Shaffer, had purchased his property from a white man.)

From this strong family environment, our mother went on to marry, a man with few of those characteristics.

Our father was a big man, with a coolness about him, that some people called a country-slick style. He loved to tell joke, flirted with women at every opportunity. Our mother, however, was more family oriented, believed in a family structured around the male provider. Unfortunately, this structure broke down not long after they left Mississippi for Chicago.

Occasionally, I heard my mother tell friends about my father's behavior, which was common among men who moved north. They could become abusive, stay out all night, have girlfriends. Some of the southern African Americans, men from the south would spend their paychecks, drinking, gambling and other vices, with little left for their families. I remember my father staying out late sometimes, coming home on payday, with very little money, for our mother to buy food, basic household items.

* * *

We didn't hear from my father very often, he would send money to us, if our grandma asked him, for his support. Grandpa would drive, Grandma to the Ralph Dexter plantation nearby. The Dexter's also owned a general store, where local families could buy household goods, purchase gasoline or get tires repaired.

I was not aware, that the Brand Plantation, and the Dexter's Plantation, were family related

Once we arrived at the Dexter home, my grandma would ask to use the phone, enter their home from the back. (I had a strong sense that my grandma and Mrs. Dexter had an unspoken respect for each other.) Mrs. Dexter, would ask the operator to make a collect long-distance call, the person on the other end, would have to accept the charges. Mrs. Dexter's, house reminded me of our apartment in Chicago, even though the house was larger.

Occasionally, I would get to speak with my father briefly, he never wrote, sent cards, on our birthdays, generally staying out of touch. Grandma, had become our protector, in every aspect of our lives, from school homework, to participation in school activities. She had a vision that some better, thing would come to us with education.

Unlike our father, our mother wrote us regularly, sending us letters with a few dollars, almost every time, and birthday cards. My grandma, insisted we write her back promptly, this was a writing activity, practice almost weekly

* * *

With the perspective gained over the years, I think my father's brother, Uncle King, may have shared some of the attitudes of our father. Otherwise, why would he leave a good job in Chicago, a wife and three children, to live with his parents in rural Mississippi? At the time, I was too young to imagine, any reason for him to do such a thing.

He had traveled to Mississippi, for what he described as a vacation, but soon afterward we learned he was staying with us. That he would do essentially, the same thing my father did, abandon his family. This again, illustrated to me, their family structure was not like that of my mother's family.

Most people in Clay County called my uncle Kang, the Muda, had a dialect of their own. The miss pronunciation of basic words. This would make thing very difficult in my English classes, all the way through my educational career.

The Muda, dialect would handicap, my ability to read, especially comprehension techniques.

In his relationship with us, Uncle Kang, was a good man who meant well, cared about us. Occasionally he would stir us up, by saying our brother Sam, was his favorite nephew. (He looked most like our father), leaving Daniel and me, out of the spotlight. In fact, Daniel looked more like the Johnsons, more than any of the rest of us. If our grandpa, became angry with Daniel, he would say, "looking, just like that Jordan Johnson." Grandma Ella, told me, I looked like her boys, if I didn't move my head fast enough, I'd get a big grandma kiss right on the mouth, on my arrival to visit her.

Uncle Kang, knew our situation wasn't very good, he believed that education would help us. (He had stayed in school longer than most, reaching the 11th grade, prior going to the army young man, that lived in Mississippi.)

Uncle Kang, bought me my first bicycle. He supported our schooling, just like our grandmother, his mother. He supported as a father, tolerant of us attending school while, other children worked in the cotton fields.

Sometimes, he would tell our grandparents how to raise children in the 1960s, he felt their approach had become outdated. Considering how much was changing in the South, elsewhere in the United States, what he said made sense to me.

We could tell this troubled him in some ways. We must have reminded him of his own children, provided him the chance to make up for abandoning them, by helping us, easing his own guilt. Uncle Kang, must have felt, how his brother abandoned us. I had heard his wife, tell our mother, that he was abusive, which I knew wasn't the right way to act.

I was the only child on the Muda, a beautiful, red bicycle. He had told me if I could pick a certain amount of cotton during the harvest, he would get me the bicycle. I did my part, he did his, which was an important lesson for experience. A side from the usual excitement of merely having a bicycle, I knew, I could ride that bicycle throughout the Muda, outside the Muda!

One afternoon , school was out for the summer, he brought a letter for me, that was written by a girl in West Point. The Muda, was so far back in the woods, the mailman, left our mail on the Highway, 2miles, away. This was the first time, I'd received a letter from a girl, so I was thrilled.

All in all, my brothers I, benefited a lot from Uncle Kang's presence. Despite his failings, he taught us about hard work, taking responsibility for yourself, supporting the family by bringing food home, other good qualities.

One winter he found a job, at the Forest Preserve planting trees. Taking a small axe with him every day, he was able to make money during a slow period, that helped us eat better, live better.

Sometimes we have to take the time, to observe people from all angles, to reach a fair conclusion about them. Uncle Kang's, presence helped us feel closer to our father, too, which was good for us emotionally.

In addition, my grandpa's brother' had sons older than us. These young men, took us under their wings, like big brothers, help us understand, expectations of daily life, in Mississippi, which we were eager to learn.

My grandpa, brother had one son, that tried me like a brother, Adam David. He was a very special cousin from cutting my hair, to telling about his dreams.

There were so many questions, I had about life, having any idea, how to get the answers. Fortunately, I found some comfort in prayer. Yes, prayer, I could feel the Holy Spirit, even when, I didn't know where it was coming from. (PRAISE GOD FOR THAT FEELING)

Belief in God, gave me a sense of protection, from the unpleasantness swirling around me. I felt peace, that God existed in me, would make things better. I was thankful God, had placed people, nearby who could look out for me, including Grandma Ella, Uncle Kang, uncle Perl and Aunt Connie. They cared for me, giving me confidence, I would not have had otherwise.

At church our grandmother, often prayed that God, would help me find my way through life. She prayed aloud, if you trust in, the Lord, he will make a way for you. Her faith, prayers and love meant so much to me, at that time. Now, my grand prayers surface in any moment, mean even more, as I enjoy getting older

* * *

It was a common practice in the South, to use first names throughout generations. For example, on my mother's; family there were four or five men named Jordan. That was a powerful name on my mother's side of her father, Jordan. Ella, was my grandmother's name, it was my mother's middle name, it seemed as if dozens of her relatives, included Ella, were in their names.

Often, the first son was named after the father, the first daughter was named after the mother.

I also learned that my mother's grandfather was a white man. As a result, some of my mother's siblings had relatively light skin. In those days, African American, with lighter skin, would find better job opportunities, than field work. (Although we were not related, there was another Watkins family. This Watkins family, could pass for white, attending our church.) Our mother and two of her siblings were not as light, reflecting their father's side of the family.

Our father's family was dark, with beautiful brown skin. In my generation, this combination of our parents, resulted in some of us resembling our father's family, others resembling our mother's family. My brother Daniel, strongly resembled our uncle Jordan.

One day our grandpa got really anger at Daniel, for some reason, angrily called him, "Jordan Johnson." Later, he would call him by that name whenever he wanted to tease him.

One day Samuel and Daniel, who were not yet old enough to help with the work, were playing at the cotton house. Daniel, thought it would be fun to play with some matches he'd found, which naturally started a fire. Although cotton burns slowly, it wasn't long before everyone could see the smoke, running toward the cotton house. We found Daniel, with burnt hair and eyebrows.

Grandpa was furious. "You look like old Jordan Johnson!" All Daniel could do was stand there, feel bad, since he was no longer a "Watkins" but a "Johnson."

Samuel, meanwhile, was a deep thinker, like many relatives, on our father's side of the family. He had a bad experience when he was very young that might have encouraged that personality trait.

When we were still in Chicago, Samuel was just a baby, he fell behind the bed one night. Our mother woke up at some point, could not find him, which scared her. Fortunately, she found him quickly, he had fallen onto a hot radiator pipe, was burned badly. For some time after that, our aunts and uncles would visit often, to help change his bandages him. I've never forgotten that frightening experience, can't even imagine the pain he must have felt from those burns.

Samuel, looked up to me, when we were in Mississippi, we rode horses, did a lot of things together. He could read better than I, his grades were better. He seemed to understand subjects easily, while I had to work hard!

Samuel and Daniel were very close, often inseparable. They were pretty adventurous, too, exploring the farm property, the surrounding the area, as country children often do.

Grandpa, called Sam little daddy, we called him big daddy, he looked so much like our father did at his age.

As the years went by, Sam realized he wanted a life anywhere but Mississippi. At one point he had a plan to ride a motorcycle to Chicago. The plan never seem to work, earning the money to buy a motorcycle.

* * *

Children were delivered by local midwives. The nearest hospital was nearly 20 miles away in West Point, Mississippi, A midwife, is a woman trained, to assist other women in childbirth. They are trained professionals, who care for mothers and their infants. They help women, have healthy pregnancies, optimal births, good recoveries during the post-partum period. Midwives, provide individualized care, unique suited, to their physical, mental, emotional, spiritual and cultural needs. However, the only time the sharecropper women would see a midwife as on the day of delivery.

The expectant mother, would be advised, comforted by her mother, mother-in-law in most instances. Miss Viola, the midwife, who my grandma, told me later in life, she had had delivered me. Miss Viola, was loved by the entire community, a beautiful salt-and-pepper hair, that was coarse, slightly braided. There was little conversation: she would speak to the mother/mother-in-law, who was with the expectant mother, then with the expectant mother directly.

My grandma, took Miss Viola, into the large room where my uncle's wife waited, for the baby's blessed arrival. In the sharecropper family, pregnancy was a family affair. Chores of the mother-to-be were shared, among the other family members, as her condition progressed. Still, as long as she could, she would chop cotton, pick cotton to the extent, that it would not harm the unborn child. Back in Chicago, I learned about a bird called the stork, which brought babies to their families. Life in the Rural Mississippi, was straight to the point, everything was so much simpler in Mississippi.

LIVING ON THE MUDA

I often think that Mr. James Thomas Brand, my grandpa, had a relationship, perhaps accommodate the both of them. While living on the Muda, my grandfather had the opportunity to move, if he wanted, purchase some land, property of his own. In my opinion, I felt that my grandpa, may have been satisfy, with the ideal, of just renting from him, as a sharecropper. Mr. James Thomas Brand, also paid my grandfather, additional funds for his service, in the order of hauling cotton, during handy man jobs in the Muda. My grandfather was a nice man, that in his eyes, he had grown very close to me, as his grandson, look at me as his son more and more. Yes, he had his own way of showing he love to me. He entrusted me a driving the prize possession, which was his pick-up truck. That pick-up truck would be the Cadillac of the rural south, the vehicle of choice.

My grandpa, went door to door peddling watermelon, in all neighborhood African Americans and whites. My grandpa, made additional money while sharecropping, anytime its rain, he would puddle something, he was always hustling making money. My grandpa always had money in his pocket. (I can remember on one occasion I found his flour-sack bag of coins, freely help myself daily. With that financial purchasing power, without been notice for having money. Nevertheless, my brother would question me, how was I able to eat in the lunchroom daily. My grandpa would sometime take me with him on his peddling route, sell the watermelon.

My Grandpa, would sometime take me with him, he would sell watermelon, it was good to go on a trip. Those watermelon trips, selling vegetable door to door, was exciting, my grandpa, was an excellent salesman. Very confident, driving up to White families, plantation owner home, as ask would ask them like purchase a watermelon.

My Grandpa, peddling watermelon, most of the time my Grandpa wouldn't peddle his fruits and vegetable on plantation properties. most Plantation African American, would raise their own food, that could be planted, grown on the plantation.

Today this was different. My grandpa went on the large plantation called Brand Town. This was the property, own by Mr. James Thomas Brand. This plantation areas, had countless of houses, everything in that area took on the name of Brand.

My Grandpa, didn't try to sell, any of his products on that particular day. He went to only he went one house on Mr. James Thomas Brand Plantation. The house had a lady, that was a younger than my Grandpa, a little boy as well younger than me. She was excited, smiling with joy to see us both. I ask my Grandpa who was that lady, normally he would indicate that was our cousin; however, this time he indicated only a friend of the family.

My Grandpa didn't take me in the house with him, left in the pick-up truck alone, was just waiting. I finally, discovered that my Grandpa, the Lady went on the side of the house, away from everyone's views. Just the lady and my grandpa on the side of the house, I stay out of view as well.

MY (3) GRAND BOYS
BY, CHARLES WATKINS, III

This is a poem I wrote about my Grandmother.
This poem is about my brothers, and I.
Daniel, Samuel, and Charles.
This also a tribute to Alice Watkins, my Grandmother.

Today, I think about my children.

I'm raise my children.

I have vision of these (3) boys, 28 years ago when their father and uncles were their ages.

I've had those Boys, in my house for 8 years

I've giving them all the love, any mother could have share for her children.

I would lay down my life to save those boys.

I've start calling them mine, using more of their father and uncle names.

I see the rebirth of my young motherhood when their father was their ages.

Regardless, how time, modernization change, the way people dress, and act.

My love for my Children and Grandchildren.

My love for them is God's love for me.

Oh God's, Oh God's how those (3) boys have kept me a young lady.

I'm proud to call them Boy's, my Boy's these are, Alice Boy' s

Thank you, Jesus.

For my (3) grand children

MY TWO GRANDMOTHERS

I live with my father's mother, had developed a bond with her, she was very kind, like my mothers. My father mother, never talked bad about my father on any occasion. My mother, would write letters to us a minimum of (1) weekly. She would, have some money, in the letter for my two brother and me. Oh, how our father mother, would place her heart in feeding clothing us. She wouldn't allow us to miss school, to work in the fields. Grandma, would insist that our Grandfather take us to visit the nearest Town, which was West Point, Mississippi, in Clay County. Upon arrival to West Point, Mississippi, the small Town everyone had the day planned out. My (2) brother, Sam and

Daniel, would always find out where Uncle Cal, our mother brother, always was near the Bank, on Saturday making his bank deposits.

Our Uncle Cal, in most situation he would give them, over 3 days' supply of work money. The money he gave, it would three days, to earn in the field around the Muda. Saturday, purchase items, as well as have fun, while in Town. My brother, was not able to hustle around the Muda area, to find work on other plantations. I had established myself, earning some money working, selling a small amount of moon shine, to some customer that my grandfather served, during his absence. My Grandfather customers, they would show up, I would allow them to purchase the moonshine from me. I measured it by the ounce and selling it to the customers around the Muda.

CHAPTER 8

SEGREGATION

For young people today, for anyone who did not live in the South years ago, it is hard to imagine, much less appreciate, the magnitude of segregation.

Coloreds and whites were governed by unwritten yet clearly understood expectations. Crossing a line could have harsh consequences.

Rules for each race were very clear. "Negroes" and "whites only" were clearly labeled on bathrooms, water fountains and restaurants. In the movie theaters, Negroes had to go in the back entrance to get to the balcony – after purchasing their tickets up front with everyone else. White people would sit on the main floor and could use the bathroom inside the theater.

My Grandpa often spoke of Emmett Till, a 14-year-old boy from Chicago, who got out of line, with an adult white woman, while visiting relatives in Money, Mississippi. He was brutally murdered in 1955. The husband and brother of the woman, accusing Emmitt till, supposedly had flirted, took it upon themselves to murder that child. He was tortured, shot in the head, eventually found in the Tallahassee River, with a heavy Cotton Gin Fan wrapped around him.

This sent a message to all African Americans boys, stay in your place or the same would happen to you. Flirting with white women was not permitted under any circumstance.

The only place that served everyone, regardless of your color, was the bank.

At the bank, Negroes could interact with white people, in a normal manner. Everyone stood in the same line to deposit or withdraw money. Since, I was a little boy, my grandpa, told me, to always stand behind him. I didn't get to close to the white women and scare anyone. He wanted us to stand six feet from the white people in line.

* * *

As more Negroes moved to the cities, and those in the South began to feel empowered, many individuals became active in their communities. There are far too many to mention all of them here, but here are a few who I felt made an impression in my life.

Phillip Randolph (1889-1979) was an important civil rights figure emerging from the labor movement. Throughout his long career, he championed black workers. He was among the first to view the black working class - not the black elite - as the major hope for black progress.

Alex Haley (1921-1992) is best known for works depicting the struggles of African Americans in Henning, Tenn. He began his writing to help pass the time during his two decades of service with the U.S. Coast Guard. After interviewing Malcolm X (1925-1965) for *Playboy*, he turned the material into his first book, the prize-winning "The Autobiography of Malcolm X," in 1965.

Malcolm X, of course, was a towering figure at that time. Born as Malcolm Little in Omaha, Neb., his father was a Baptist minister, his mother watched over eight children. He rose to prominence as a member of the Nation of Islam. He gained further stature after leaving that organization, visiting Mecca and becoming an articulate, forceful advocate for people of all races. Tragically, he was murdered by three Nation of Islam members.

Althea Gibson was the first great African-American player in women's tennis. Raised primarily in Harlem, she won a string of American Tennis Association Titles, on the African American Circuit, before being invited to major tournaments. She became the first black player to win the English (Wimbledon), French and U. S. Open titles. Gibson turned professional in 1959 and later made more history by becoming the first black player on the Women's Pro Golf Tour in 1960.

She became one of my favorite athletes because as a tennis instructor myself, I have encouraged minorities to get involved with these sports. The United States Tennis Association, the United States Golf Association, grant financial support to encourage minority to get involved. Both organizations have donated millions of dollars to better minorities in tennis and golf.

Sports is a great training ground for adulthood and citizenship. It provides a structure in which you can develop particular skills. Sports, building self-esteem, as people say today. Being part of an organized group working toward a common goal, experiencing teamwork also give youngsters, a framework for growing into productive adults.

*   *   *

The struggle that Negroes had started from Negroes, to Blacks now African-American, or People of Color, this is why I wrote this book. My experiences occurred in the late 1950s and early 1960s, when blacks were called Negroes. This book was written using the term Negroes. (Changing Negroes, to African American.)

CHAPTER 9

SHARECROPPERS FARMERS

My grandparents, was responsible for 16 acres of farmland.

Just a few months earlier, I had been in a big city with beautiful buildings, nice cars, well-dressed people, stores everywhere; Now, I'm living and working on 16 acres. Fortunately, living on a farm meant spending most of your time working on the farm. We could feel more like ourselves when we were working.

Farm work, it was hard work, we got up very early.

Waking up in the morning, was a challenge, as many nights, we didn't sleep so well on the cotton-stuffed mattresses. Mostly, evenings it was still hot and muggy, which didn't help. We didn't have house shoes, there were no rugs on the floors and most days we wore the same clothes.

But we woke up, got up every morning, washing our faces and hands in a pan, with a bucket of water nearby to replenish the pan if needed. "Everybody washes your hands and face to get ready to eat; now I'm not going to say it again." Our grandma, would call out, she never said this a second time, you knew this was your only chance.

As my grandmother made breakfast, I could smell the fat back pork meat cooking on the wood-burning stove. I knew the morning menu by heart: cane syrup, rice, salmon patties, homemade biscuits, eggs, milk and coffee.

I didn't like our unpasteurized milk, though, I thought it was not clean. Every time I saw it on the table, I couldn't forget, the image of my grandpa washing the entire cow udder, with the same water every day. To my city sensibilities, it just wasn't right!

After breakfast, we all would walk to the fields, knowing we had a long day ahead of us. Most days, you didn't want to be the last family entering the cotton field, as there was friendly competition to avoid being last.

My grandma would work in the cotton field with us, once she thought it was an hour prior to stopping for lunch she would walk back to the house and start cooking our lunch. She would do the same thing, at the end of the day.

I can remember asking myself, why, I'm in the cotton fields? I had been living with my parents in Chicago, a beautiful, exciting town. Now, I'm just working in these hot, dusty cotton fields. I could not understand how the vacation, I expected became indentured servitude.

*   *   *

Milking the cows, was a challenge for me under the best of circumstances, you could be downright dangerous, if the cow was cranky. Every time, I milked that cow, I thought about the good taste of grocery store milk, which reminded me, I was a city boy who belonged in the city.

The cow, had to be tied to a sturdy post, the teat washed with warm water. You'd place a bucket underneath the udders, then sit or squat in a position, that would enable you to move quickly. Next, you'd apply a lubricant on your hands, wrap your hands around two of the four teats, squeeze both of the teats and direct the milk into the bucket. Then you'd repeat with the other two teats until they looked deflated.

*   *   *

When I got to be about 12, my grandma decided, it was all right for me, to find work outside our usual chores on our own field. A few times, I worked with my grandma, her friend chopping cotton on another plantation, which was smaller than ours. At the end of that day, the landowner paid my grandma and her friend $3 for their work, while he only paid me $2. (He said I couldn't work as fast as the adults.)

Most of the time, working on other plantations was paid by the day. Mr. Ralph Dexter's plantation would hire groups of people, mostly younger people, from the James Thomas Brand, plantation and pay $2.50 or $3 per person, for the day. (If it rained at some point, though, you would get paid only for the work you had done to that point.)

Mr. Dexter also owned the community grocery store, that had gasoline and fresh groceries. The people who worked for him, were allowed to get credit against their wages for lunch, other things they might need. (For example, Mr. Dexter, would have tickets for lunch and other things you had purchased. The amount of credit, was based on how much money he owed you, for the work you were doing. You couldn't get cash but you could get food or other items.

*   *   *

Grandpa, always had a hustle on the side, like selling moonshine whiskey or peddling watermelons. Most every morning, I could see my grandpa drink a little white lightning directly out of a gallon jug.

Our grandma, would sell eggs, to the local grocery store, which was about 10 miles from our house. We would take the family truck. Other times, she would sell livestock for extra money.

As I live today, find a great deal of those value in eating, cooking, and the use of my hands. Those survival skills, took from the Muda, displayed in my heart, have aid me in the rough time of my live. The only ways that you can survival the difficult time, you need to have been in a mineral [similar?] environment to aid you in difficult time. (For example, the lack of money, the cost of employment.) The

Muda, was a simple way of life, farming, fishing, and hunting… That would allow you to sustain and foundation of living and survival. Nevertheless, very little attention was toward the improvement of the living quarter in which the people lived in, provide shelter for the sharecropper.

While living in rural West Point, Mississippi

Living in rural Clay County, I learned about living. In my mind, I called it the circle of life. Living in the rural everything appears as it is, in that circle. Example: People are animal this how it works, you breed you conceived, you're born and then you die. However, we are as human civilized animal with moral mentality and survival skills; We have the instinct, to take care of our families in under all circumstances, that nature or life difficulties present to us. This is my value that has lingered in my mind and my soul, by being a young boy, in rural Clay County, Mississippi.

The heart of man doesn't know what "God", for those who love him, what I'm persuaded. My strong belief in "God", so many aspects at any aspiration, that he as restored up my soul. God, in difficult times, he would show his mercy, by giving you guidance. "Hope will rescue you, by giving the circumstance to "God", he would work it out for you, if you truly have that faith." This song in an old Negro spiritual song.

Rural African Americans, value is what I'm talking about.

CHAPTER 10

HOME LIFE, LEISURE TIME

Life in the country was best lived simply.

If you worked the land before planting the seeds, and had good weather, you would have a good crop yield. Many years later, seeing the movie "Lion King" reminded me of the animals' breeding periods and births, the fundamental element of nature's cycle.

The landowner recently had built a new barn, where he would store corn and hay for the livestock; we kept our livestock in a fenced-in area behind our house. There also was a fenced-in area connected to the barn; We milk our cows and feed them, we would feed the hogs, store our work mules, during the summer, keep them fed and healthy.

Most sharecropper families, had gardens for their own food, in addition to the livestock. Popular foods to plant included sweet potatoes (which could be baked, mashed, oven-roasted with onions, or maple roasted) and white potatoes (including Russet, red and petite). One of the most popular food groups was greens: mustard greens, turnip greens and collard greens (with corn bread, of course).

Many hunted and fished, to provide additional food for the family dinner table. Hunting, was especially important in the winter. Our grandpa, would bring home rabbits, raccoons, opossums, deer and squirrels. It was very common to see a raccoon or an opossum as the main course on Sunday's dining room table.

The enjoyment of snacks, we made our own: There were no convenience stores, selling potato chips of beef jerky. We had the opportunity to grow, make almost anything we wanted. Some of my favorite including; peanuts; pecans; sweet potatoes; pork skins; small pieces of pork belly; black walnuts; cookies; pies with berries, peaches and pecans; cakes including chocolate, coconut, caramel, gooey butter and pound cakes; sweet tea, sometimes coffee; hominy corn; and roasted green corn. All of these snacks tasted good and, for the most part, were good for you as well.

Many families also grew some corn to sell, splitting the proceeds 50-50 with the landowner.

* * *

We used mules, for many tasks, which tractors are used today. Mules are hard-working, they knew not to overwork themselves, put themselves in dangerous situations. This is why many people call them stubborn.

Besides food and water, the mule needed a harness, to pull a plow or wagon. The harness, consisted of a breast collar, reins, bit, girth and the trace or tug. With its padded strap running around the chest, the breast collar is sufficient for light duty.

*   *   *

One unfortunate fact of country life back then, was that there were few doctors to care for the sick animal and people. Family and friends had care for the elderly. As we know, people didn't live as long under these circumstances.

Some sharecroppers, had burial insurance, but most had none. Typically, bodies were buried in pine boxes covered with white cloth and a white flower. The dirt covering the grave would settle after a few rains, as there was no caretaker for the graveyard. (Volunteers would dig the graves.) The undertakers, Funeral Directors, would provide a metal marker to identify where the person was buried. So, few people could afford grave Headstones, only these simple markers memorialized the deceased.

Churches didn't keep up with the burial plots and over time graveyards would be abandoned. Families didn't go out to visit the graveyards, which were just fields, unlike White Cemeteries, there were large Headstones reflecting the families,' financial means, to show pride in the deceased.

After the funeral, family members would search the home, for whatever valuables and keepsakes they wanted. Unlike today, few people had photographs of the deceased so those keepsakes weren't to be found.

*   *   *

Most people seemed to enjoy the simple life, which was just as well. There weren't as many leisure opportunities, as there are today. You had to find your own ways, to have fun or occupy your time.

Both adults and children enjoyed music. The record player, that was one of our sources of entertainment. My uncle, had purchased the player, when he lived with us, we loved to listen, most of our leisure time.

The first record, I heard was, "Don't Cry No More", by Bobby Blue Bland. When those blues singers belted out their songs, our grandma, lost all of her religious, like a juke joint person, we'd never seen before. She was transformed by the music.

Sam Cooke was one of my favorites, "Let the Good Times Roll", was among his early hits. Sam Cooke, was a songwriter, singer and successful entrepreneur. His distinctive voice and stature in the music made him a role model, not just another entertainer.

On the radio, we would only hear country music, I grew up enjoyed, as time went by. I enjoyed hearing George Jones sing, "Homecoming in Heaven," Johnny Cash sing "Ring of Fire" as well as several other artists. During my years in the South, the radio stations didn't play African American songs on the radio. You could hear African Americans records, at home or in local nightspots known as juke joints. These were informal establishments, featuring music, dancing, gambling and drinking.

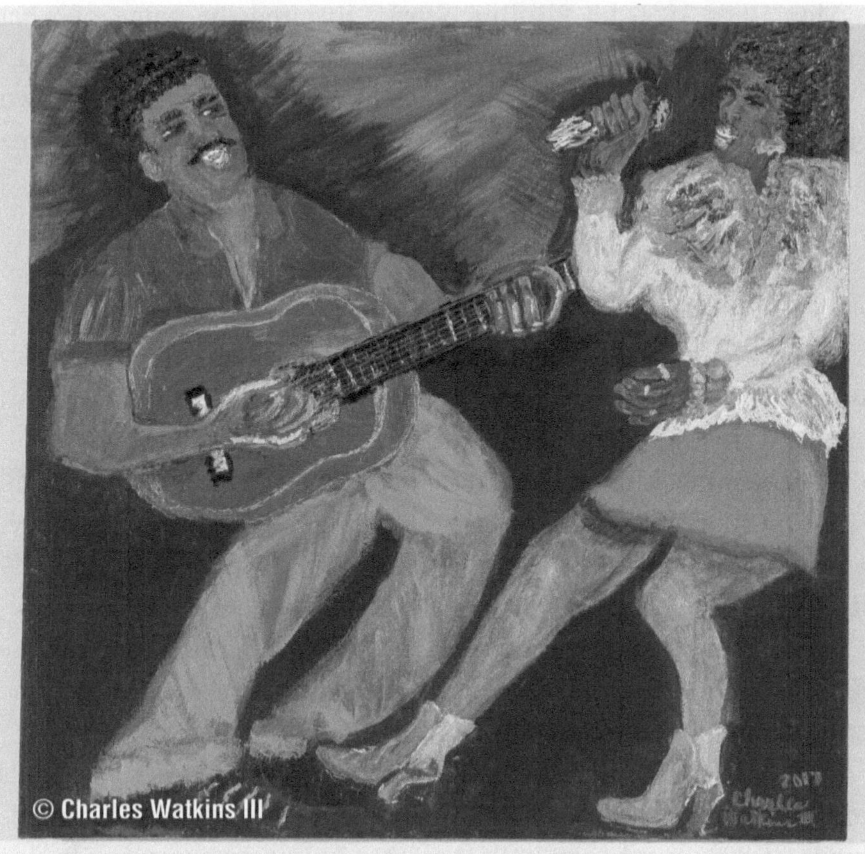

There were many African Americans blues artists, of the day, most of whom grew up in the South. The recording artists, recorded in Chicago. Most found success through their records and performances, going on Tours. They gain wider audience, they began to reach urban white people. White musicians, in England, who embraced, they began their own careers playing these songs. The Animals, Cream, Fleetwood Mac and the Rolling Stones all began by covering blues songs by Howling' Wolf, Muddy Waters, Willie Dixon and others.

Muddy Waters, born McKinley Morganfield in 1915, in Rolling Fork, Miss., also moved to Chicago and eventually signed with Chess. He, too, had a string of hits such as "Baby, Please Don't Go," "Can't Lose What You Isn't Never Had," "Hoche Cochise Man" and "I'm a Man." His 1950 hit "Rollin' Stone" inspired the name of what eventually billed itself as "the greatest rock and roll band in the world."

Although Willie Dixon, was a well-known musician, in his own right, his greatest fame came as a songwriter, whose songs became huge hits for Howling' Wolf, Muddy Waters and others.

* * *

The smaller towns didn't have juke joints, where illegal whisky was sold, there were no packaged liquor stores. The beverages of choice were moonshine whiskey and home brew.

Moonshine, often called white lightning, mountain dew, hooch, home brew or white whiskey, had a high alcohol content. Moonshine, essentially is an unaged whiskey, clear with a hint of corn. Usually it was substituted for store-bought whiskey in cocktails.

There are many varieties of moonshine, depending on the distillation process, the number of times, the spirit runs through the still, the individual moonshiner.

Moonshine, has been around for centuries, we can trace its origins to the Appalachian region. (For example, Tennessee moonshine, is made of 80% local corn with the other ingredients varying by the moonshiner. Cooking corn turns the starches, into fermentable sugar. Add yeast to mash to transfer the fermentation process. Breaking the natural sugar into alcohol, after three to four days the mash is transferred into the pot still. The mash is heated; vapor travels into the thump key and rises again. The vapor is condensed in to a liquid, with the moonshine approximately 150 proof (75% alcohol).

Bootleggers sold moonshine out of homes mostly, and sometimes through juke joints. Most of the time, the bootlegger would purchase gallons of liquor from the moonshiner and then sell bottles of it to juke joints and other retailers at a wholesale cost. Individuals would purchase liquor a few ounces or a drink at a time.

A bootlegging retailer would throw parties in their homes, mostly on Saturday nights because the sharecroppers stopped working at noon Saturday and did not work on Sundays. At the bootlegger parties, men would gather to flirt with women or just get drunk with their friends.

Drinking moonshine was common. It was an established activity among the men, and some of the young boys observed the drinking, which led some of the young men to share their moonshine with the boys to get them started on it.

There were few alternative activities – there weren't any libraries, for instance.

* * *

Like children everywhere, we found games we liked to play.

Sometimes, my brothers and I, would play four-hole marbles under the house, where it was cool. Four holes were made about three feet apart in a straight row. The object of the game was to go shoot the marble in every hole, one at a time, without missing a hole; if you missed a hole the next player could knock your marble out of the way and you would have to start over. The first person gets back to the starting point would win

Other games we played included:

- Hide and seek. We played this at night in the barn, when you found someone, who was hiding, you would have a small bucket of water to pour on them. That person would then hunt for others who were hiding. This would continue until the last person was discovered – and wet!

- Oil Fire Ball wrapped in Rags, would be tied together, to create a large ball, sometimes as large as a 16" softball. The ball would be soaked in kerosene (then called coal oil) and we'd play catch with them at night. The idea was to catch, throw the ball, before it burned your hands. It was dangerous, of course, but beautiful to watch. Coal oil was common then, and used for all sorts of things around the home. These included treatment for many ailments, including coughs, cuts and scrapes. It is a shale oil that is distilled from cannel coal, mineral wax or bituminous shale, used most often for lamps.

- Rabbit hunting with sticks. Any kind of stick was acceptable, from broomsticks, shovel sticks, axe handles, etc. Dogs, would locate the rabbits, once the rabbits started running the aim was to throw the stick at them. Often the dogs would find a rabbit would just sit still, so we couldn't find them or see them.
- Raccoon hunting. We hunted raccoons at night, with hound dogs that had a strong sense of smell. Finding the fresh scent of a raccoon, the hound dog took off, running to find the raccoons. This required us to run hard, to keep up with the dogs. It could last for hours until, the dogs were able to chase a raccoon up a tree. The dogs would remain at the base of the tree until we got there. Sometimes, it seemed as if the dogs were talking to us, as they made it clear, that the raccoon was up in the tree. This was exhausting but a lot of fun.

- Fishing. There always were people, who would fish all day, come back with something,
- to eat.
- Fishing, was to catch food, not just relax or have fun. The fish you caught, was cleaned and eaten; catch-and-release was not a part of the program.

- Riding mules and horses. The same mule that pulled the plow, during the day, could take you for a pleasure ride later, they provided good transportation even if they weren't fancy or fast. It was much better than walking. Some families in our community were horse trainers, had horses that were very fast. These horses had shoes and saddles, unlike the mules that were ridden bareback, could compare with any horse in the area, regardless of the owners' color. My brother Sam and I, loved to ride horses several times, we got into serious trouble, with our grandpa. We would get caught for taking a ride without permission, or for getting caught in a rainstorm.
- Baseball was played in a pasture or meadow, and all ages played together.
- Gathering nuts was popular in the fall. Wild pecans and walnuts fell to the ground and you could collect quite a few

to sell or eat. Some plantations, had pecan orchards where you'd find a line of wild pecan trees with a variety of pecans. Sometimes we'd climb the trees and shake them or just use sticks to knock the pecans down.

- Swimming in the creek. Skinny-dipping was the practice since none of us had swimming trunks. The water tended to be muddy, which often would leave a dirty residue.

*   *   *

Our grandma, wasn't too happy, when we came home from the creek, she reminded us often that we should stay as clean as possible, even though we had no bath or shower. Every night, she would fill up a pan in the sink to wash our underwear. Towels were washed only occasionally.

CHAPTER 11

CHURCH

Sunday was the day of rest for the sharecroppers. It was a day of rest everyone observed.

Our grandparents took us to Robinson Baptist Church, about 5 miles away. Most community activities, including funerals, baptisms, Sunday school, and revivals, were held there, as is the case at most country churches.

On Sunday, church was an all-day activity. You would get of bed as early as possible to start cleaning your body from head to toe. Everyone in the household followed this routine because Sunday was the day everyone put on their best clothes. Most people didn't have much money, on Sunday everyone looked like they did. Your appearance did not reflect where you lived, where you had come from or anything else.

Sunday, was an opportunity for rural fathers and mothers, would show off, how well they were doing, to show off their daughters, who at the ages of 14 and 15, were preparing for courtship.

Going to church on Sunday, was one of the highlights of Mississippi, life for me. I enjoyed seeing those real cute girls (whose parents kept a tight watch on them, not letting them out of their sight). I could tell the girls were just as excited to see the boys.

Sunday school, started the day for children. Some of the children could read extremely well. Most had a southern accent and spoke with a southern drawl.

From about 10 a.m. to 4 p.m., there would be a visiting minister from Tupelo, or another small nearby town. This minister, would receive an offering from the congregation, and at some point, during the day a member, would prepare a nice Sunday, meal for him and his wife.

The service would begin with a lot of singing and praying, clapping and foot-stomping. The congregation would pray for their children and other relatives who had departed this world or had gone up North. After what seemed like a long time, the preacher would preach. The sermons usually were very interesting, with the only variation being which day of the week the preacher was saved from being a sinner.

The talent of some of the children, sang in church was amazing. You could only believe, how good they were, you were right there watching them. many of the adults could sing very well.

Every summer, the church would have a weeklong revival. This would start off by having the children from ages 10 to 13, sit on a bench or pew, at the front of the church. It was called a mourner bench, and intended for mourners or repentant sinners seeking salvation.

The congregation, would pray that God, would save them from their sins, forgive them of their sins. There would be a great deal of preaching, singing that would last all week, conclude on Sunday, with a baptism of the new Christians.

The mourner's bench, was a ringside seat on the best preaching, singing for miles around. All week long, there was praising, singing, hand-clapping and foot-stomping. The congregation, made its worship music with voice, hands and feet.

Following tradition, grandparents would call out their grandchildren's names during the praying. The children, would be crying, the family members would tell them the only thing. God would make two steps, all in Jesus' name.

Some mourners bench participants, would come off on the first day of the revival, some on the last day. There always were a few who didn't come off the bench at all, those children had to return to the mourners bench the next year.

* * *

The revival was held in the "Laid Back Time" of late summer. This was when the cotton plants, were the cotton so large, that the weeds couldn't harm the plants. We would not have much work to do, until we began in September, to gear up for harvest. Nearly everyone enjoyed the "Laid Back Time."

* * *

My grandma, informed me that she was going, to take me to the mourner bench, to discover god, confess my sins to god, the Son of

God, which is Jesus Christ. My grandma, said, its time that you find out the power of God. This introduction to the mourner bench, would be, my first step in a personal relationship with God. I knew the mourner bench, would be some special, a personal step in becoming a young adult in the church for you boys and girls at the age of 12 to 15 years of ages. This was a step that the children, would make a public announcement, in the rural part of Clay County, Christian, which most people had done prior to me becoming a candidate to go in front of the general public to solidified that. I believed that Jesus was the son, of the most holy God, that all their sins, would be washed away, by his holy faith. Just believe in God, confessing publicly that you had been born again, by leaving your past on the mourners' bench.

The children discover, the power to find the lord God, peace in themselves. I didn't know the power that followed prayer, until it was my opportunity to visit that rural Robinson Baptist Church mourner bench, in Clay County, Mississippi. On that big day, that hot summer day, it was my turn to attend. The mourner bench would have two services, for those that participated, those in the prayer services. The mourner bench participants, would be schedule to report about 11:00 am, for the first morning service, again that night for service at 7:30 pm. The first service would be mostly women, children participants; most of the men would be during some type of work outside job to make extra money. There would also be (1) Quest speaker, that would conduct the convention service.

The summer days, would be hot and the convention, would last for 7 days, which would take place in late July, early August for the services. These Baptist conventions, would be live and active. Once the cotton plants, growth were considered the maturity of the plant, where the weeds couldn't take the nutrition, from the soil of the cotton plants. The cotton field, were a display of blooms, squares, and leaves. The beautiful field, white and red bloom that could be seen, blooms covered all the roads of blooms everywhere. This display the bloom garden, of the cotton field. If you ever seen picture, of grapes vines plantation, rows in Napa Valley California, vines growing in individual rows – the reasons were primarily for cultivation (at first to protect the vines from weeds this for cultivation and for harvesting upon).

This period for the cotton process, that enable the sharecroppers to take time off from continue chopping weeds, from around the cotton plants. The heat of the hot summer, would allow the cotton plants to fully develop the Cotton Bowl, prior to the cotton getting ready to go to market for processing at the Cotton Gin. These hot summers, would be where, churches would have church convention. The teaching of the blessing of God, how to pray. The time, parents would renew their faith, the word of God. I want all readers just to picture those Cotton Fields, the rows of cotton; Picture those beautiful blooms everywhere, as far as eyes could take in for that moment. During this time in late July, the cotton fields were actually at its most vulnerable where the Squares and Blooms, on the Cotton Plants, couldn't be disturbed. Every little square on the branches, would become a cotton bowl. In the late July and August, the cotton had grown from 1 inch as a seed to plant two now the small seed is now a 4 feet mature plant in early July. (Let me add the sum of the cotton plants would grow as high as 5 to 6 feet at the totally maturity stage. The rows on the cotton it would be drain system to take the water away from the plant and wouldn't allow [standing?] water.

I want the readers, to get the feel of, how wide the Sharecroppers, had all this time to go to one of the Baptist conventions, to participate in all that singing, praying, the cotton plants in the crops, were always the main priority. All phases, of the growth of the cotton, from the seeds, to the last cotton and pick out, of the cotton field. Mourner bench, time was also when the women in the communities would get together and socialize participate in the local 4H clubs, arts and crafts. This would be a time when small farmer landowner African American farm Women, would come to the church to socialize as well. Socializing interacting with each other my grandma love to do with her neighbors.

As I have elaborated that the cultivation of the cotton, gardens were vital part of the sharecropper survival for their family. I want the readers, to have a visual part in see them on the plantations. The terms that were used back during that particular time lay-by or laid-back, time for the cotton to go through the final stage, of opening up, prior to cotton picking time. Every flower had a cotton boll under it.

Yes, we know now why the Sharecroppers, had time for the mourners' bench. Let's discuss the spiritual significance of the mourner bench. My grandma, only said that, I would be going to the mourner bench, that summer only once. She, didn't make any preparation, with me to attend that mourner bench. The only thing she said, I would be going now. I look back at that mourner bench situation, in Clay County, it was like a summer camp, Bible class -- children getting educated about, God in all aspects. This was also time for testimony, from all farmer that would tell the congregation, all their blessing that God, had provided for them.

This journey to Robinson Baptist church mourner bench, would change my life, would give me another spirituality look on life. The dressing was casual, nevertheless very serious once I enter the church. On that mourner bench, the church environment became very serious for the children, that would be attending that mourner bench. The emotions were very intense, with not any kidding around from any of the children's, that were in the church or seat on that mourner bench. Parents, would pray out, aloud for the children's asking God to come into their lives. The children sitting on the morning bench, would be the entire church concern, with singing, praying that old-time religion, for the mourner bench candidates, while everybody would join in with the best gospel singing from miles around. This celebration, it was only for the children to have a transformative, from being a sinner, to born-again Christian.

The children, would characteristic, were very serious, that was the entire climate of the church, the mission of the elders in the church. Everybody praises God. With continuously singing and praying, one by one parents would start up a new song, praying aloud after the song. Hand clapping, foot stomping in church, good old fashion religions, to save those children, asking all of us that were on the morning bench, to make one step of faith. God, is my savior just by walking off that morning bench, give your hand to one of the adults, that stood there in front of you singing and praying, for God to save you. Some children came off the bench, on the first night of the prayer meeting; I didn't move however. I continue to pray and sing to myself without anyone seeing my mouth moving. Oh, I begin to hunger for my soul to be saved and experienced.

I had heard my grandma and grandpa praying, while working in the cotton fields. I've heard my grandpa praying out aloud, while just during chores around the house, in church services on Sunday. I would quietly, walk in the room sometime, I would hear her crying, she didn't know that I was present in the room in which she was humble asking God to bless her family, humble asking God, to watch over her children and grandchildren. This would go on for 10 to 15 minutes without her really noticing me present, while making my journey on the mourner bench to find God to forgive me, for my sins and save my soul. The first few night while, I sit on that mourning bench, with all those other children the praying, it had all of us crying, with that emotion that spilled over into that entire congregation of the small church named Robinson Baptist. My grandma, had become more serious looking at me by now, asked me was I praying to God, about saving my soul. I had never seen that look on her face, with a concern for me.

However, expressing the love of God, she had trust in the Lord, how door would be open just living a righteous life, how door would be open. All my life, while a little boy in Chicago, prior to coming to Mississippi, I knew God, I didn't know as my grandma knew God. Nevertheless, I knew my god, that was deep inside of me, I talk with in time of need. During my time in Chicago, sometime our mother didn't have money, I have found money in the street while in Chicago, at the amusement park, on that roller coaster ride. That drop down 100 feet or more after climbing to the top of the amusement park, just drop down all at once. I've always had something inside of me, that told me that regardless. Whenever, I called on him, for his help during my difficult time, I was never alone, feeling deep inside of me, the core of my body. This little Faith, that I had in me was growing larger and larger. God, could see my transformation into the trust in God, love for me. I knew that, I had an invisible friend that appeared.

Today would be my third night on the mourners' bench. Tonight, is a Wednesday. My grandma is looking very serious around the house I can see praying very deep in thought. As we leave that old house going to Robinson Church, I'm getting my mind ready for all the singing and praying that would take place tonight. We had no clocks on the wall in that old church – we didn't have any agenda. The only things that you could plan on were good where ship for that night and preaching to follow. The weekly conventions the adjoined community around the area, including some peoples off of Mr. J. T. Brand larger community plantation you could count on seeing people that had vehicles to come and give their support to the convention that we held.

My grandma, would take on a leading position, this night, the singing, praying for the member of Robinson that night. The church opens, with flair, look like everybody that night, was talking to directly to me, about my trust in our Lord savior. It was now, the mourners to get on their knees pray during prayer time. I didn't know it, would be my grandma praying, the mourners got on their knees, prior to the person that decided to pray for the sinners', forgiveness. To step out of faith, take the hands of anybody, that were present standing up at the revival in church. I was ashamed to get up, walk toward my grandma. I trust God, Shame just covered my body, this was my reason for stay on the mourner bench. I wanted to trust God, take a hand as my Lord and Savior. I believe that, I had been born again, in the faith of good. Stop all my sinner ways, start living a righteous life, turn to God, for his wisdom guidance to support me, be better person in the sight of God.

Once, I discovered my grandma, was the person that was praying, for all of us, just asking God, to help us to find our way, to his mercy love, please give us the courage to trust in him. As my grandma prayed, she brings [began?] to take it to a higher intensive level, with her voice, humbleness in her praying. Once. I thought that my grandma had finished, her prayer, I thought, I had escaped the message that she was asking God to help us, my grandma, went deeper into her prayer deeper in her voice, start calling out my name. My grandma had now started praying for me in front of the whole church. My grandma had connected me to God, I could the

Holy spirit, with her prayer. She had washed all the fear, the shame, that I had, pertaining to stepping off of that mourner bench. I'm on my knees praying. I'm copying off the prayer that the other people had prayed for me, just by repeating their prayer as they pray. I'm now strong in my faith, I'm not ashamed to say "yes I love God – I believe Jesus Christ died for our sin," this was a clear feeling that I could live with, for the [rest of my life?].

I couldn't any longer stay on that mourner's bench. I had contact, with God directly, all those feeling that. I had inside of me, when I was worry, it was my prayer that, I had been praying. However, didn't understand who, what was giving me this wonderful feeling.

CHAPTER 12

MY LIVESTOCK

While living on the farm, my grandma gave me livestock, for my very own. Owning livestock, property, was a form of wealth, livestock always could be sold for cash, so naturally, I felt wealthy indeed.

My herd grew from one pig (a sow) to four (her three offspring). My grandparents told me, I was to raise them for an eventual sale; they were not kidding.

Of course, I thought the pigs were fun, and continued to treat them as pets. My grandma, had given me the three pigs', mother as a piglet,now she had three piglets of her own, all of them continuing to grow.

I made sure the three pigs were very well fed. All three had distinguishing marks on their bodies, distinguishing enough as far as, I was concerned.

The younger three pigs were black, with white spots, that looked like islands in a sea of shiny black hair. They looked ready for a 4-H Club competition!

(4-H, is a leading nationwide organization, providing positive youth development, youth mentoring, serving six million young people from ages 5 to 19. In partnership, with more than 100 universities, 4-H groups are active all over the United States. The group's motto is "to make the best better.")

You could tell these pigs were not ordinary farm animals, they were so clean and shiny; most pigs preferred mud and lots of it.

Sometimes, I would, use the four-hole marble area, under the house to feed my pet pigs. I would, put corn in the hole, that we had for our marble games. I also made the mistake of feeding them from my hands, so they would follow me around like puppies, begging for food corn they, knew I carried in my pockets.

my grandma, called me into the house, asked me what was my planned to do with the pigs. She said, the pigs would grow into hogs, pet hogs couldn't be in the house, as they would eat almost anything. Domestic hogs rarely look for their own food, would eat as much as 5% of their body weight a day. [SOURCE]. After our conversation, I knew, I would have to plan for the pigs' sale. I couldn't let them be farm pets, problems for my grandparents, for other farms, if they got loose.

There was a white man, who came into the area, now then to purchase, trade livestock. My grandpa, said I was getting too much powerful, owning so much livestock, my grandma stood strong on her decision, that the pigs were mine. She said, I could keep all the money from selling them. (I decided I would give my grandma a portion of the profit.) The white man came around, grandpa allowed me to sell them. I sold only two of the pigs, I could keep my favorite, despite all my grandma had told me, might occur if I kept a pet pig.

Well, one afternoon I heard a pig squealing, off in the distance. I didn't bother to investigate right away, it turned out she had wandered off, to another homestead, the people were not aware, she was a pet pig; all they saw was a stray hog on their property. Their sheepdog had chewed up one of the pig's hind legs, pigs have a different circulation system, with few veins in that area, the damage wasn't permanent.

I nursed that pig back to health, sold her to the same man, who purchased the other two pigs.

* * *

My management of the three pigs, was not the first time, I didn't follow directions, not treat the livestock as pets. One spring, our grandpa, bought a goat, for us to eat on July 4. When we had family arriving for the big holiday. After my grandfather, told me we would raise the goat and then it would be slaughtered, for the feast, naturally, I befriended it.

The goat, became close very quickly, I was the one who fed him. I had looked into his eyes, he looked into my mine. He liked all the corn, I had been feeding him, since my grandpa raised him for slaughtering.

On the morning of the holiday, I was awakened by the crying of an animal – I thought it was a dream, then realized it wasn't. My grandpa, had that goat hanging up on a tree, and his throat was slit, he could be skinned to be cooked, for the holiday meal. I cried, cried.

My grandpa's friend, laughing, asked him if he killed my pet for the holiday. My grandpa said, I knew full well, what was going to happen. I started crying again, which made my grandpa mad.

Although cooked goat meat smelled very good, I just couldn't bring myself to eat my friend's flesh. I think I finally had a goat sandwich, after everything quieted down. I didn't want to keep the pig around, for that reason. After seeing what happened to that poor goat, I didn't want to be any part of hog-killing. Once they were gone, I didn't have to worry about what happened to them.

* * *

Bryan Brothers Packing Co. was a meatpacking processor in West Point, Mississippi, It provided income for many African Americans, in the area, many of whom had Good jobs there. This work could be part-time, in addition to Sharecropping, full-time if the worker wanted to get off the plantation.

The older Sharecroppers, didn't seek other employment, to avoid drawing attention to themselves. All the plantation owners, talked among themselves regularly, and word could travel fast.

My mother, had two brothers who worked their way up the ranks at Bryan Packing Company, from the killing floor. My uncles, Cal and Perl Johnson, left the farm moved into West Point, eventually becoming leaders in the community. My uncles worked hard and were good providers for their families. Uncle Cal, who was a hard worker, married a nurse, her father was a respected Doctor. Uncle Perl married, the West Point High School music director, who also served as music director, for several local churches.

I will talk about my uncles later in the book. Their stories will be tied in with the story of my extended family.

CHAPTER 13

GRANDPA'S PICKUP TRUCK

Our Grandpa always had a good pickup; this was his means of traveling, the area selling his vegetables, watermelon and moonshine. Many times, he had the opportunity to buy pickup trucks, from the two main landowners on the Muda, James Thomas Brand and James Wade.

Grandpa, never was a big spender on anything in particular, except to purchase a good pickup truck. In fact, his pickup usually was one of the better pickup trucks, in the area. Whenever, I asked Grandpa for money, he said had very little; he answered our grandma the same way, whenever she asked.

Our Grandpa, hauled cotton for other people, who lived on the Muda. He hauled Cotton, to the Cotton Gin.

As I grew older, I became very interested in driving that pickup truck. Whenever, I was with him, I'd watch Grandpa, start the motor, and shift the lever on the steering column.

Many times, I would get in the truck and start the motor for him. I had learned how to start the motor from watching my Grandpa. I didn't have any idea, how to operate the gearshift. The gearshift, was on the steering column. I knew this would take some time, and practice to master.

One day, I hopped in the truck sat in the driver's seat, my grandpa came outside. This was the beginning of my journey driving on the MUDA.

When my grandpa came out of the house, he could see, I was sitting in the driver's seat, and not the passenger seat. As he walked up, I started the engine. He smiled so brightly and asked me to move it; I had no idea, what to do since, I couldn't put the truck in gear. All those times in the past, I had watched my grandpa, start the truck, put it in gear, take our Cotton to the Cotton Gin, yet I did not really understand what he was doing.

After this experience, he showed me how to shift the gears, let me practice driving around the neighborhood.

Soon it was time for me to show my grandpa, that I knew all the elements of shifting.

To get first gear, I made sure I wasn't touching the gas pedal, then pressed on the clutch pedal, pulled the shift lever toward me. Then, I carefully let out the clutch to engage the gear without, disrupting the engine. Second gear, was in the opposite direction, again shifting after letting off the gas and pushing in the clutch. Again, letting the clutch out smoothly was important. Third gear was a little easier, as the lever moved straight down (toward the floor).

Reverse was entirely different from, the three forward gears. To get into reverse, I had to make sure the vehicle was stopped, press the clutch pedal, pull the lever all the way toward my chest, let the clutch out, even more carefully than before.

Once I showed my grandpa, I could drive the truck, operate the gearshift properly, I knew he, saw me as a driver.

My grandpa, would allow me to ride with him to the Cotton Gin, to get the 1,200 pounds of Cotton to be processed. After riding with him several times, I asked him, could drive the truck back home. He always was proud to see me learn, other tasks, that would help him around the farm. While there were older boys, around who drove the family truck, none starting doing so as young as I was.

One day, I was driving around, near our home, drove over some speed bumps that were on one of the roads. I was going too fast for the speed bumps fell out of the pickup truck, which kept going, ran into our neighbor's hen house. To make matters worse, on this day, I had not asked (let alone received) permission to drive the truck.

Fortunately, the neighbor's wife and my grandma had been best of friends since, long before I was born. (I was still in trouble, though.)

Soon after that episode, I was assigned to take the Cotton from storage shed, load it in the pickup truck and then drive the 10 miles to the Cotton Gin. I started selling watermelons, too.

CHAPTER 14

ROLLING STORES

Most landowners, had tenants on their farms, properties who had little, no cash until the end of the work year. Nevertheless, the tenants could get basic food items from the land owner's dry goods store on credit. This credit, would be recorded, then subtracted at the end of the year, after all the Cotton was harvested, from the cotton fields.

The landowners', stores only had basic food items, such as meat, flour, cake mix and various household items. There wasn't much available to provide nutrition. Only the men could go the dry goods store, since the Patriarchy, gave him domain over all items in the home. I liked going to the dry goods store, it had candy and Moon Pies.

Country peddlers, also visited from time to time. They did not have much variety of items to sell, everyone in the neighborhood, would try to purchase something from the peddler, they wanted him to continue coming around.

In Rural areas such as ours, 10 miles to the nearest store selling fresh bread, many residents didn't have any way to travel that distance. Often, people bartered with each other to, get things they wanted. The Sharecroppers, usually succeeded in obtaining what they wanted.

Fortunately, Rolling Stores, met the needs of many rural families, who were spread out, unable to get to the landowners' stores. Several companies operated converted trucks over many routes.

One Tuesday, it had started raining. Grandma, had just left the Cotton Field, to go home, make our lunch. Grandpa, continued plowing with the mules to prevent the weeds from growing well enough to threaten the Cotton Crop. With June and July being so hot, I always looked forward to rain.

When it rains enough to get the ground wet, tilling isn't successful, the moisture in the soil helps replant the weeds. By the time, I got to the house for lunch, I realized it had rained enough, that we wouldn't return to the fields that afternoon. The Rolling Store, making its regular stop the next day, I could start getting ready for that treat.

The Rolling Store, would appear on our old dirt road, I remember hearing, "Candy, potato chips, soft drinks, 10 cents!" With 50 cents, you could purchase a piece of heaven from the Rolling Store. As soon as the Rolling Store, stopped, the driver would open up the doors. Some adults would purchase chewing tobacco or loose tobacco to roll their own cigarettes.

Meanwhile, I'm excited, I've saved money aside, for a shopping extravaganza! I had earned my coins by helping neighbors, selling pecans, anything else, I could find, I could buy a Baby Ruth candy bar, a box of Cracker Jack or Stage Plant cookies.

Mobile Stores, had traveled Rural areas for years, I came along. It was a creation that could bring, chocolate candy, cookies and warmth to my heart. I loved seeing it, travel down the dirt road, with a cloud of dust behind it.

(Between those Wednesdays when the Rolling Store visited, my grandma sold candy. While it couldn't compare with the variety found in the rolling store, it was a last resort to help youngsters' sugar craving. My grandma, would hide the candy to prevent my two brothers and me from eating the candy or even selling it ourselves.)

That Rolling Store, would park on the top of the hill, not far from our house. All the houses in that area, were old, looked like old, dried wooden houses, that should be torn down, else renovated at great expense. Nonetheless, these houses were well designed, constructed – just not maintained.

Just as, I finished some of my chores around the farm, the Rolling Store would show up, everyone would see it and head toward it. While standing in line patiently, one by one the customers would tell the store owner what they wanted. The Children would play around the old truck, knowing they had sufficient funds, to buy themselves a treat.

One day, suddenly, a child noticed smoke coming from one of the homes. That smoke quickly became a roaring fire – it seemed a lot like a tornado to me. It's already burning, the flames combined with the blazing sun, made everything nearby feel like part of the fire.

One of the neighbors said, gasping, "I left my child asleep, on the bed! Please help me get my baby out of the house." As our neighbor ran over 100 yards, to reach the burning house, everyone could see the flames, smoke coming through the front door, and windows. As we approached the house, the roar of the fire increased along, with white smoke mixing into the dark gray smoke. Now, we hear the baby crying, most of us looked helpless. Several men attempted, to enter the house, could not get past the flames and smoke.

Worse, the only water pump was more than 75 yards away. It was obvious almost immediately, that the pump would be no use in saving that mother's house and baby – there simply was no provision for this kind of catastrophe.

Hopelessness, despair gripped the onlookers as the smoke, fire engulfed, the entire house within minutes. Before long, the crying stopped and the fire burned the house down before dying down on its own. All of us, realized we had witnessed the baby's death. Tears, flowed from the mother's eyes over the loss of her little boy. Everyone around her had their own pain, as well, after seeing the heartless fire tear through that old house.

Only God could ease the mother's pain, which would remain with her, for the rest of her life. I know God, had heard that baby cry, it came to such a sudden stop. I prayed that peace could be with that mother and child, that God's love might comfort her in the days, months and years ahead.

CHAPTER 15

RANDOM OBSERVATIONS

My brothers and I felt a little different from the other children; we had lived in the north. We had seen and done things most children on the farm or plantation would never see or do. Most plantation workers knew very little about the outside world. We could not understand why our parents would have us live with our grandparents.

So many things seemed strange to us, or not right. Coming from the big city, we couldn't help but notice that many children did not have much in the way of clothes, and hardly any shoes. In the summer, most children went barefoot.

I knew I wouldn't stay in Mississippi all my life. I decided I would leave at the first opportunity. Someday I would be back in Chicago, where I could dream again and make a new start. I prayed a lot about this, as I didn't want to stay there and settle for what the others had.

* * *

Almost, every Saturday my grandparents, would go to the nearest town, West Point, Mississippi, a 45-minute trip. Visiting West Point, often was the highlight of my week.

The African American, who lived in West Point, were different from those of us in the rural areas. That was mainly, the African American, in the city had established themselves, better, enjoyed more economic stability, of the different industries in the town.

Sometimes, we would visit my grandma's best friend Magnolia and her husband, named Mr. Lieutenant (the rank he held in the Army). Mrs. Magnolia occasionally served homemade beer or moonshine. She and my grandma, often would talk about their sons, who had left Mississippi to go north.

It was amazed to me, how much some parents had sacrificed for their own time, energy to help their children, move north while they remained in, West Point, to continue Sharecropping. The parents knew, they had to continue meeting all the obligations, they had despite losing a key worker. The parents remained, accountable for the cultivation, care and harvesting of the Cotton.

The landowner, already had determined, the amount of land, based on the number of people living in the home. The departing offspring there would be fewer people, to do the work. Many, like my grandparents, were getting older.

It seemed that quite, a few young people who had left, Mississippi did not send any money, back to their parents. The parents, who remained behind, the youth who left didn't seem to have any plan. Once the young people were settled, a plan to help the parents, who expected to be Sharecropping, right up to their final days on God's beautiful Earth.

The young people who moved north, were generally between 18 and 25 years old. They felt none of the responsibility to the landowner that their parents did. In many instances, the plantation owner didn't even know children, have moved away, until weeks or months later. (The children very seldom came back to visit their parents.)

Most of these young people would leave at night, so no one could tell the plantation owner or their families. They also might do this to avoid conflict, with those who stayed behind. I now, know the plantation owners, were aware of the great migration north - they were educated, knew their business.

We'd also visit Uncle Perl and Aunt Connie, who I always enjoyed seeing.

Uncle Perl, was a supervisor at Bryan's Packing Company, (meat packing company) , my aunt was a respected music teacher, at the high school, at local churches. Strangers, looked at you and treated you differently, when you were with people such as my aunt and uncle.

Southern schools were segregated then, and the African American Teachers, were especially strict, not tolerating any unacceptable behavior. As far as they were concerned, if you were in school you were there to learn; if you didn't want to learn, then go back to the cotton fields.

One time, they invited me to spend the weekend, with them. It was an outstanding experience, right out of a television show, of their very different status in the community. That weekend, was very special, I told my grandma, how much, I enjoyed spending time with, my mother, her brother wife, and their small son, Ricky.

I always loved visiting with them, I was careful not to tell others about it. African American, back on the plantation already knew about my mother's family, were jealous. which made me worry they would start saying I was uppity (a word often used to describe people who were aloof, snobby or acted as, if they were better than anyone else). Anyone with a reputation as uppity would have trouble with African Americans as well as white people.

*　*　*

The first things, when people came back to West Point, Mississippi, from the north, were their appearance. They looked different from, all of us around, West Point, both rural and city. It was, the indoor plumbing they had, they could take baths every day, stay out of the harsh weather. The contrast was remarkable. The people from the north looked cleaner and brighter, some young men would have their hair straightened.

*　*　*

Most of the African American, took pride in whatever they did. Regardless, whether they were sharecroppers, landowners, businessmen, farmers or regular workers, that pride in their work was obvious to me.

*　*　*

One of the things our Grandpa, always emphasized was common sense. Common sense, many people today joke, isn't as common as it was back then, is the practice of two perceiving and judging things in the same way sensible people would judge them.

*   *   *

Not all rural Mississippi, African Americans, went to moonshine houses, juke joints to pass the time. In addition to those going to school, many young men entered the armed forces.

For decades, a wide variety of social and ethnic groups, including African-Americans, Hispanic-Americans, Asian-Americans, women and homosexuals, were generally limited in entering military service. However, thousands of African-Americans served with distinction from the Civil War through the present day.

After the Civil War, the Army maintained four Regular Army regiments for African American, the 9th and 10th Cavalry and the 24th and 25th Infantry. These men often were descendants of the Civil War soldiers, who fought in these regiments.

Most African Americans communities, had several honored men of the Grand Army of the Republic who had served their country well. Retired infantry and cavalry sergeants often were leading citizens in their communities. The 369th Infantry, characterized by some as "possessing black skins, white souls and red blood," silencing the claim that Negroes were cowards and would not fight.

Claims of cowardice, were not the only insults African Americans faced. Indeed, often African American troops, were abused by their white officers. In France during World War I, white American officers attempted to import the worst features of color. African American troops were deployed as shock troops, entering the most dangerous war zones and being assigned to the hardest labor. In July 1948, WWI veteran President Harry Truman issued an executive order desegregating the U.S. Armed Services, but it wasn't until combat realities of the Korean War sunk in that the military became fully integrated a few years afterward.

*   *   *

Here are a few thoughts for you to consider.

> *Sharecroppers' lives were limited; don't limit yours.*

> *What do you have in your life's plan? Break the chain of poverty. Be the exception to other people.*

> *Don't let your gifts and confidence fall into a rut.*

> *A seldom visit makes a better friend.*

These Bible verses provided me a great deal of comfort.

> *For even when we were with you, we gave you this rule: If man will not work, he shall not eat.*

2 Thessalonians 3:10

> *Eye has not seen, nor ear heard nor have entered into the heart of man things which God has prepared for those who love Him.*

1 Corinthians 2:9 (New King James Version)

> *For I am persuaded that eighter death nor life, nor angels nor principalities nor power, nor things present nor things to come, nor height nor depth, nor any other created thing shall be able to separate us from the love of God, which is in Christ Jesus our Lord.*

Romans 8:38-39 (New King James Version)

CHAPTER 16

EDUCATION IN CLAY COUNTY AND MISSISSIPPI

As you'll recall, my early education in Mississippi, was limited to a one-room schoolhouse. However, there were quite a few excellent educational institutions in our area.

For a while, I attended Fifth Street High School in West Point. We were bused to and from school and our driver was Mr. Jefferson. He had several children of his own, and often they rode the bus with us. In the main hallway, Fifth Street High photographs of past senior classes. There was a large photo of my uncle Sam's class from many years earlier; I liked knowing that he, my mother, another uncle was looking down on me from those class photos.

Mary Holmes Seminary College, in West Point, was one of the most beautiful places in the area for African Americans to be educated. As I observed, the African Americans children, walking on campus with pride, not having to work in the Cotton Field, reminded me of what I often saw back in Chicago. Rev. Mead Holmes wanted, a place where his daughter could attend school, and his vision was realized in 1892 by the Board of Mission for Freedmen of the Presbyterian Church, which founded and managed the school in its early years in Jackson, Miss. They opened up with the initial objective of training young African American women, to become homemakers as well as leaders in the community and church. The students there were primary school through high school.

Three years after it opened, on land donated by local African American citizens, the school burned down in 1895. It then reopened at a new campus of 20 acres on the outskirts of West Point. The school suffered another fire in 1899 but reopened the next year.

The early curriculum focused on three areas: Literature, Music and Industrial. These included courses in grammar, history, science, math, Bible studies and Practice (domestic arts). In 1932, it became a co-educational institution and focused on training school teachers for Negro communities. This was a change taking place in other southern African American colleges at that time.

In 1959, the state assumed responsibility for K-12 education. In 1969, the school changed its name to Mary Holmes Junior College, was no longer under the direction of the Presbyterian Church. It later became Mary Holmes College.

In 1991, the main building on the West Point campus was added to the National Register of Historic Places. (Sadly, the school closed in 2005.)

Mary Holmes Seminary, was an inspiration for me whenever we passed the campus in Grandpa's pickup truck. This reminded me, that not everyone lived and worked as sharecroppers.

Over the years, I had noticed that not everyone took pride in getting educated, not settling for less. For me, passing by Mary Holmes Seminary, motivated me to do better, to lead a better life, get back to the city. It made me determined to work hard, overcoming any disadvantage I encountered. This is what, I felt seeing the well-groomed youngsters walking around the campus. I could see the possibilities education provided.

* * *

There are quite a few African American schools, with distinguished histories. Howard, Hampton and Fish were founded by union generals. Lincoln University in Missouri was established after the Civil War with funds given by enlisted men of a regiment of the

U.S. Colored Troops. Before the Spanish-American War, Wilberforce in Ohio was the only African American colleges, with a department of military training to which Army instructors were assigned.

Alcorn College (now Alcorn State University) in Loman, Mississippi, is another one. It was established in 1871 to educate freedmen. It has many prominent graduates, including author Alex Haley and football player Steve McNair.

Medgar Wiley Evers, is another graduate. He entered Alcorn in 1948, studying business administration. He played football, ran track, and participated in choir and debate. He earned his bachelors of arts degree in 1952, not long after marrying classmate Myrtle Beasley. Together they had three children.

Evers later helped organize the Regional Council of Negro Leadership (RCNL) for a boycott of gasoline stations that denied Negroes access to restrooms.

In 1954, he applied to the segregated University of Mississippi law school, which rejected his application due to his race. That same year, he became the NAACP's first field secretary for Mississippi. A few years later he was involved in James Meredith's efforts to enroll at the University of Mississippi. Evers also organized the Biloxi wade-in protests against segregated beaches on Mississippi's Gulf Coast.

Medgar Evers fought hard for Negro equality, contributing to countless social advances in the 1950s and early 1960s. On June 12, 1963, prior to pulling into his driveway, Evers was struck in the back by a bullet that ripped through his heart. He was taken to a hospital in Jackson, Miss. Initially he was refused treatment; however, 50 minutes later he died.

Earlier that same day, President Kennedy had called for the end of Jim Crow laws.

CHAPTER 17

RETURNING TO CHICAGO

In the summer of 1965, our father told our grandparents that he was coming down for the July 4 holiday. We thought sure he would take us back with him this time. Recalling how, I came to be in Mississippi years earlier, I became very upset and cried. I did not like living on the plantation, saw no future in it. Even visiting my aunt and uncle in West Point, which was so enjoyable and relaxing, felt like a long distance from the farm.

After our father arrived in his sky blue 1961 Oldsmobile, my brothers and I felt sure we were headed back north. We were so excited! Considering how all our neighbors liked to gossip, we knew our friends would hear about it but not really have any idea of city life. Like most youngsters, all they would know was that we had gone away.

Our father, was not very talkative this weekend, never saying a word about where we would live. At one point earlier he had indicated he would find a larger apartment or house, which is why he said he couldn't keep us in Chicago. He had married a woman named Ida, who would become our stepmother. She was distant emotionally, not at all like our own mother or the adult southern women we had come to know.

After these eight years, I was still mad at our father for lying to us and leaving us here. This July we would leave after the holiday weekend, leave behind the poverty of the Muda and find what was sure to be a better life. We were so happy to be leaving, I didn't care about my livestock or any other personal belongings. I didn't want anything to hold me back or tie me back to this farm life. We would be able to go to school and concentrate on getting an education that would improve our lives.

To our disappointment, however, our father drove back to Chicago after the holiday weekend. He promised to come back, but didn't say when.

So, we resumed our usual summer of hard work in the cotton fields. After our bubble of hope was burst in July, it seemed like the sun was hotter, the work harder and the days longer. So, we looked forward to starting school again in the fall.

By this time we had begun riding a bus to school in West Point, because Abbott School, which started as a one-room schoolhouse but had grown into a building with a room for each grade (K-12), suffered from grounds that became so muddy after heavy rains that it was dangerous for anyone to try getting in or out of the building. The ground was flat, did not drain well, and there wasn't much grass even in the best of times. The area also had a lot of limestone nearby, which magnified the sun's brightness into a blinding light. It was not an environment conducive to learning or much of anything else.

While attending Abbott, my friend Aaron Shelton taught me how to carve figures in the limestone. He was a wonderful friend and a talented artist, like the rest of his family. Aaron and I would spend time at the limestone finding just the right place where water would stream down. It was easy to find suitable pieces of limestone, some as big as your hand. A pocket knife was the only tool we needed to create our latest masterpieces. (Everybody carried pocket knives back then.)

Finally, the first day of school arrived. We caught the bus, rode to school. To our surprise, the teacher told us we could not attend class. She sent us to the principal, who told us we could not go to school there anymore. Our grandparents had to pick us up.

Given our grandma's strong belief in education, she got to the bottom of this in no time. A law had been passed, over the summer made children living with their grandparents no longer able to attend local schools. I didn't realize immediate, this new law was my ticket home!

Grandma called, our father right away, he realized he had no choice but to take us back to Chicago so we could go to school.

Grandma gathered my two brothers and me and told us we were returning to Chicago, but that it would not be what we expected. There were things about Chicago, and about life, that we were too young to understand. That would make it even harder for us to readjust to the big city.

At the same time, she said it could be a chance to take our lives in different directions. It was up to us to make the most of it. To help us with the transition, she planned to go with us and stay for a while until we were settled.

Our older cousins, Adam David and Willie, came by to see us after they heard the news. They understood why we were leaving, still were sorry to see us go.

For me, I knew I had earned a reputation as an outstanding worker, a teenager who could work as hard as any man. By the time I was 15, I fully supported myself with the various jobs I had, buying my own clothes and other essentials. All the plantation owners and black property owners knew me. It was up to me to earn respect all over again.

My vague memories of Chicago, probably wouldn't be of much help, as I was seven years older and had matured quite a bit. Regardless, I was certain Chicago would be far better than a rundown old house on a plantation in rural Mississippi.

Despite the struggles growing up there, my grandmother's love was so important for this small boy who felt abandoned by his parents. Her love for me, and the love I felt for her, is still with me today and it comforted me as we got ready to leave.

Leaving before just harvest time, my brothers and I, realized we wouldn't receive any money from the year's cotton crop. Before the law changed, I had put my school clothes for the fall on lay-away, so I'd have to write the store and send payment from Chicago. This was a disappointment, naturally, but a small price to pay for getting back home.

We left at night, of course. There were six of us in the car: our father, our grandmother, my two brothers, my sister Ella, and me. It reminded me of the trip down there, when I didn't know what was going on. This time, however, I knew all night long that we were driving away from one way of life to reach another.

Having made the adjustment to farm life in Mississippi, I was confident, I could overcome any challenge and seize any opportunity. I was able to dream as a 15-year-old, not as a man expected to perform back-breaking work on a plantation. In Chicago, no one would care how well I could chop cotton, or load a truck, or bale hay. (At least on a farm you never were homeless or hungry – food always was available.) My mind began focusing on what I could achieve in Chicago: the opportunities were unlimited.

I felt more in control of myself on this trip, much more aware of the world around me. In Memphis (about one-third of way to Chicago), I could see the changes in how African American were treated. There were no "whites only" or "colored" signs for the bathrooms; white people were more friendly than they had been in the past. It wasn't that way in rural Mississippi, where I had barely stepped out of Clay County.

In Mississippi, and all over the south, some African American, had begun protesting over civil rights and voting rights with the help of the Freedom Riders. Sharecroppers, however, did not protest about anything; they were focused on working the land as hard as they could so as not be in debt after the harvest.

We wondered whether, we would ever return to Mississippi, for any reason, or work for food and shelter on a farm. It was clear to us, that a limited education led to limited opportunities.

As the years went by, I became more aware of the severe poverty surrounding the Sharecroppers. My grandparents' house, was so rundown and shabby it was obvious. We were poor, just like everyone around us, not held in much regard by others.

We recognized that education, was the key to our futures. My brothers and I, could focus on growing up, learning without having to prove that we were big, strong men. There were other ways young people should show their power, such as getting educated. We were fortunate that the Fifth Street High School, had outstanding male female teachers, who inspired us.

With each mile toward Chicago, only God knew the relief I felt. The 700-mile journey was the first part of my transition to adulthood. Now, I was like so many who had migrated north before me, expecting a much better life. Now it was my turn to make those dreams come true.

As we drove into the city, I was struck by how organized everything seemed. People were dressed well and hurrying to get somewhere; others stood patiently at bus stops waiting the Chicago Transit Authority Bus, they needed; some stood on the sidewalks talking; everyone had a purpose for going somewhere or being somewhere. They spoke easily, articulating their thoughts comfortably. I enjoyed listening to all the conversations.

Once we reached our neighborhood, I felt like an outsider. My Mississippi farm clothes didn't look so good in Chicago – the other boys were stylish, dressed like golfers and very well groomed. They took pride in their appearance. Back then, no one wore the athletic shoes that are so common today: leather street shoes were the norm. If anyone had a gym shoe then, it was the Converse Chuck Taylor All-Star model worn by nearly all professional basketball players then, from Wilt Chamberlain to Jerry West. And they were worn in the gym, not outside.

Young men in Chicago dressed to a much higher standard, than those in rural Mississippi. Our blue jeans and track shoes just didn't cut it. The Chicago standard called for Ivy League attire, such as well-tailored trousers with cuffs resting atop fine dress shoes, buttoned-down shirts, loafers with tassels or winged-tip shoes. Stacy Adams, calfskin shoes were popular, out of my price range. I was no longer able to earn money, from the side jobs like before. I felt bad, I was dependent on my father 's support for clothing and other expenses, which of course included my brothers.

This style of clothes was considered reflective of successful people, people with futures (such as graduates of Ivy League universities). Young men wearing those clothes aspired to success, and made a strong impression in public. However, it was not a positive everywhere.

In the rougher neighborhoods, such clothing made you a target. Most young men in these parts of the city preferred what was called the gagster look, an early form of what is known today as the gangster look. Young men dressed in gagster fashion could go anywhere in Chicago without concern. Gagsters indicated their gang affiliation by the color of their hat bands. The Black Stone Rangers were one of the stronger gangs then, continuing for several years.

Growing up, the students at Mary Holmes Junior College in West Point, gave me the only impression, I had of how college students dressed. Even though, I was not the best student back in Mississippi. I knew one day, I'd have the opportunity to attend college.

We lived with our father on 70th Street on the South Side, near the Chicago Teachers College that occupied three blocks on South Stewart Avenue (68th Street to 70th Street). There were many buildings, beautiful trees and manicured lawns. CTC was integrated, too.

Our nearest school, Yale Elementary School, was only four blocks away. Yale had classes for kindergarten through eighth grade, so my brothers would attend there. After that, students attended ninth grade at the Yale Upper Grade Center, which would be my school. From there, students went to Parker High School, which also had a beautiful campus. I thought this was great that we could live on 70th Street and walk to elementary school, high school and college – all in one neighborhood! This was totally different from Mississippi.

This area was a great area for learning, with the schools and black businesses everywhere, along with well-maintained apartment buildings and bus transportation to everywhere. Even though our apartment was small, we lived in a beautiful part of Chicago.

Everywhere we went we would see the teacher's college students walking to class, catching the CTA buses, all of them dressed neatly to attend class on their attractive campus. I could see myself attending college in that kind of setting.

*   *   *

We considered ourselves fortunate not to be living in a rundown old sharecropper house any longer, but our new home was not exactly comfortable.

My father hadn't made any adjustment for accommodating more people. We moved into the small, one-room apartment – seven of us, including my grandma – where Ida and my father had lived the last few years. Even though my brothers and I slept on the floor, it was better than being on the plantation.

Our grandmother's prediction that Chicago might not turn out as we expected was correct. Once again, her wisdom was right on the money.

Plus, she must have known more about Ida than she let on. Before we were taken to Mississippi, our father had moved out of the apartment where the seven of us lived and started living with Ida. She didn't have any children of her own, and she didn't have any with our father. She had lived in Chicago all her life and was very well spoken but not very caring. Southern women cared more about you on a personal level.

As our father had directed us, we called our mother shortly after arriving in Chicago. We were excited by how pleased she was. She had married again, too, and her husband's name was Kermit Nixon. He was an Air Force veteran. (I had met him just before we left for Mississippi but hadn't seen him since then.) We had not met our new sisters, Dianne and Jean, and Jean's twin brother, Dean.

We were surprised to find that our mother lived in one of the nicest areas on the South Side, an integrated neighborhood with all the amenities anyone could want.

Looking back, I came to understand my father better, since I saw him in a fatherly role for the first time, since I was a small boy. In those early years, he was still married to our mother. Now children, were reunited with him in Chicago, I saw how much time and effort it required to raise children.

* * *

The 1965-66 Chicago school year, was a few weeks along by the time we arrived, so we had some catching up to do. Much like our first school days in Mississippi, it was another culture shock for us. Being behind in the class material was bad enough, but our southern accents and southern clothing marked us as country bumpkins. We had a hard time at first.

It wasn't long before we were surprised, to learn that many of our teachers, had lived in the south, which was fortunate for us. They understood the challenges we faced. A teacher from Kentucky, found out I was from Mississippi, and asked me to take a certain seat in the classroom, so I could see him better he could see me. He took a shine to me, helped me adjust, to the new school as well as learning my subjects.

Ancient history was a favorite, it seemed most ancient people were farmers, I had lived the farming life. I enjoyed art class, too, particularly when we studied sculpture. Math class was all right, I had a lot of trouble with English. In my Mississippi school, there just hadn't been much attention to formal English.

There were a lot of new friends to make, two of my closest friends were Duane and Michael, who lived east of the busy Dan Ryan Expressway. (We lived west of the Dan Ryan.) Their families lived in a high-rise apartment building on 73rd Street, which was a littler nicer neighborhood than ours.

Even so, eventually I found out Duane, Michael and some of my other friends were in different gang territory. Some of the parents made their boys, take martial arts classes to protect themselves, which made me realize how dangerous it could be. Fortunately, I had learned a few things about boxing over the years. The gang members, respected my ability. (It helped that many of them thought I had come from the reform school out in St. Charles, Ill., where I would have learned how to be a tough guy.) As I walking down the street, with Duane and a few others, when some gang members snuck up and jumped us. Once they recognized me, they left me alone, Duane made like Bruce Lee with a handful of them and they ran off.

I could see gang life was a dead end. My dad was concerned when I stopped seeing my friends, when I explained they were in gangs, he understood.

It was clear that athletics offered, a way to avoid the chance of gang trouble. Once I started high school at Parker High, I tried out for what I thought was the junior varsity football team, soon learned it was the varsity. When the list of students making the team was posted, I was one of only two sophomores!

Our coaches were white, had attended well-known universities. They liked me, I was polite and kept plugging away, whatever they directed me to do. While, I didn't get a lot of playing time that first year, I learned a lot during our practices.

As was common back then, some of the teachers had athletic backgrounds and would assist the coaches. During my junior year, one of those assistants was a substitute teacher who had played pro football, a man named Roy Curry. Having had to stop playing professionally because of a hamstring injury, he was younger than the full-time coaches. Most important, especially for me, he had been a great athlete who knew how to lead teams and win games. This man changed my life.

Roy Curry grew up in Clarksdale, Miss., and became a star quarterback in high school. He earned a scholarship from Jackson State University, becoming the first of many great players at the school. (Throughout the 1960s, many southern universities were legally segregated or made little effort to recruit black players. Today, players of his ability are recruited from schools nationwide.) He was drafted by the Pittsburgh Steelers in 1963, who made him a wide receiver. Unfortunately, he pulled a hamstring late that season which continued to bother him the next season. Trying out for the Bears in 1965, he re-injured the hamstring in training camp, decided to retire. He played again briefly in the 1966 season but then turned his energy to coaching, through which he has guided hundreds of young athletes over the years.

Not long after, I met him, he put me through a series of drills to evaluate me as a football player. It gave him (and me) a good idea of what I did well, where I could improve. One area of improvement was speed, so he recommended I join the track team (along with a few other players). Coach Curry knew what he was doing, by the next fall I was much faster than I had been – it made a big difference in my performance as a running back, I earned my letters in both track and football. By my senior year, I was the team's leading scorer; I also played safety on defense, was just okay at that position. Our team won its division, which gave me a lot of confidence, as I finished my senior year.

I also gained confidence in a professional sense, as I had worked at a Frito-Lay plant during my last two summers of high school. The plant manager, took an interest in me, I was able to work part-time during the school year, too. This was great experience for me, working in big plant operated by a large, successful company.

After I graduated, I was contacted by several schools, Coach Curry, urged me to attend Jackson State. He knew the football program first-hand, and also knew there would be a good environment for me to learn.

Coach Curry's, strong recommendation meant a lot to me, of course, and it helped I was familiar with Mississippi. In a sense, I would be returning to my family roots, not as Sharecropper, as a athletic college student!

* * *

Black colleges, in those days promised their athletes they would graduate, did everything they could to help them succeed academically. For one thing, we went to school year-round, only able to go home at Christmas-time, a couple of weeks during the summer. We also practiced on our own, much of the year, since college athletic regulations, were much stricter than regarding the amount of official team practices.

I felt good that all the best black athletes, went to schools such as Jackson State because the Southeastern Conference weren't recruiting African Americans. Like many other small southern colleges and universities, Jackson State didn't even have a gym yet, just a warehouse with weights and stuff. The showers were in an old army barracks. We had to provide our own underwear, shoes and such – the school only provided uniforms and helmets. Some of the guys had wives and children, which really caught my attention.

My friend Duane also decided to attend Jackson State, and fortunately they had a place for us to live. We felt like outsiders because we brought nice clothes to wear, forgetting how hot it was down there. The other students dressed down so they could stay comfortable. Many of the students were veterans returning from Viet Nam.

The football environment was a shock, too. Now, I was playing with men, not high school kids. Many of the Viet Nam vets tried out for the team, too, those guys were tough. The contact was brutal, as every player wanted to prove himself for the new head coach. I felt lucky to make the team.

Most of the coaches, learned that "north" meant north of Memphis, which wasn't really all that far. Of course, I told the coaches, I had lived in Mississippi, for eight years, they acted like they didn't believe me. It helped a lot that Coach Curry, had trained us so well on the fundamentals – before long the "north" subject didn't come up much.

Often, we practiced at night because of the heat, we had two-practice days only one practice was during the day. I was fortunate that our head coach, Bob Hill, had been a running back, when he was in college, he coached us running backs directly.

Staying fit is important for any sport, but especially for contact sports. Being in shape, strong and flexible helps your performance and reduces the chance of injury – even for athletes not playing in the Mississippi heat. This, too, helped me in other ways.

One of the Academic Physiology instructor, decided there should be a physical fitness survey, to identify that athlete, who was most physically fit. We all went through a lot of drills and tests as part of this survey. The first time, I was tested, I was among the top 50; I kept working to improve myself and the next time I was in the top 20, then the top 5, eventually the most fit athlete as, I entered my junior year. The coaches asked him to develop physical fitness program to help the other athletes develop themselves, which gave me the opportunity to work with almost everyone in the athletic program. I helped a lot of my teammates and the coaches liked that I took on the responsibility.

Most of the time, I played on special teams, unlike my roommate, who was the starting quarterback. I did score several touchdowns during a spring game one year, though.

Practice was another story, as I was in motion all the time then. Coaches picked me to be a running back, for the scout team, I had to learn all the plays, of the team, we would play on Saturday, then help the defense get ready. I knew learning the other teams' plays, would keep me from getting cut.

Although my friend Duane, eventually stopped playing ball, went home, before long there were three other players from Chicago.

In those days, you had to prove yourself, to become a starter, most starters were juniors and seniors, most of them very, very good at their positions. Even so, as I approached my junior year, I felt pretty good about my chances to be a starting running back.

My hopes were dashed, though, when two particular freshmen made the team right away. One of them was named Ricky Young; the other freshman was senior Eddie Payton's little brother, Walter. Ricky and Walter were very good, they made the first team right away. It was easy to see, they had great things ahead of them.

Ricky, who grew up in Mobile, Ala., went on to play nine seasons in the NFL, three with the Chargers and six with the Vikings. In his first season with the Vikings, he led the leg in receptions.

Walter was born in Columbia, Miss., and didn't try out for football, in High School, he didn't want to compete with Eddie. Instead, he ran track and played in the marching band. After Eddie graduated from High School, the football coach asked Walter, to play Football, which he did. Obviously, he caught on fast! Walter, had a great High School career.

After rushing for more than 3,500 yards in four seasons at Jackson State, he was drafted fourth overall in 1975 by the Chicago Bears and played 13 seasons with the team (only missing one game). Walter led the league in rushing five straight years, and set many records. After seeing him work so hard with Bears teams that weren't all that strong in those early years, I was thrilled to see the Bears add enough players of similar talent that Walter could enjoy a Super Bowl victory before retiring in 1987.

The Jackson State athletic program grew and improved while I was in school. A new activity center, which had just started construction when I arrived, was now open and a tremendous upgrade from that old warehouse.

*　*　*

Football was important to me, obviously, but so was getting an education and our coaches always kept an eye on our grades. Over time, more and more professionals (holding doctoral degrees) were hired to teach us physical education students, the area most athletes studied. These smart and educated instructors and professors demanded the best performance, from all their other students. It was a great feeling to experience their passion for teaching, helping us prepare for life after college.

I was fortunate, to find Dr. Joan Campbell, who helped me as a tutor, taught me, how to write. She was not African-American, and not even from the South.

Dr. Campbell worked with me throughout my time, at Jackson State, doing so as a volunteer. I have no doubt, that God led me to this dedicated teacher, who helped me build a strong foundation, that has served, this Sharecropper, Grandson, well ever since.

From Dr. Campbell, I learned to describe personal experiences, regardless of whether the experiences, were encouraging or discouraging, to commit them to paper in ways that entertained or pleased the reader. She told me to find my own writing style, run with it, a crucial building block, in the foundation that has served, me well ever since.

I have no doubt that God, led me to this dedicated teacher. She was a bright, caring person, who helped me navigate, the academic, social environments found on any campus. By the time I graduated, I saw her as a parent, sister and friend all rolled into one.

Having long considered football a way to stay out of trouble, get a good education. I committed myself, to the educational side just like I did to football. I signed up for 18 hours of class every semester, and graduated in just over three years. When, I wasn't in class, on the playing fields, I worked nights, at the local United Parcel Service facility. The spending money was good, but the good impression, I made as a part-time worker, helped me get hired full-time as a driver after graduation. I drove a UPS package car (never call them "trucks") for three years, then served for a while as a Teamsters shop steward, became a manager – eight years altogether.

Even though, I wasn't so far away geographically, from my grandparents' sharecropper plantation, my life was headed in a very different and better direction.

I thank God, for allowing to spend those years, with my grandparents. I learned so much about life from them, which shaped the person, I am today.

My experiences in West Point, Mississippi, helped prepare me for anything that life might have in store for me. I learned about hard work, about being poor, about the value of education. Knowing how bad, life can be, keeps you focused on how, good you want your life to be. Never lose sight of your goal!

Parker High school located at 68th, Stewart street in Chicago. This was the High School, which I attend, which change my life, allow me to dream about the achievement, the transformation of the sharecropper's grandson, to a real Chicagoan young man. While at attending the junior high school Yale upper grader center. I had established myself with friends that lived across the Dan Ryan Highway, which was another territory for gang territorial people my age. These children was upper middle-class black people, the carried themselves in a different way compare to the area which I lived on 70th and Normal Avenue (off of 68th St.) The friends I had were not welcome to the neighborhood in on 68th and Stewart St. this cause disruption, once they know where my friends lived across the Dan Ryan. The gang, which developed in my neighborhood, knew me well. I was a good boxer, could handle myself very well, in the neighborhood. Parker High, went from sophomore, junior, and senior only. This school change my life; as a graduated Freshman, I had tried out for the football play. Now, I'm entering Parker High, sophomore, a part of the varsity football play, would be on a City of Chicago Blue Conference football team. Sophomores, that had made the team: Harmon Robinson and myself. He was a much better of an athlete, than I , he had grown up that way. This football team was well coached, had discipline that, I had never experience prior to becoming a part of that varsity football team. All positions were well representative by well-trained athletes.

In the High school in West Point, Mississippi, would have had the opportunity to play sport, all the children on "the Muda" had to work in the cotton fields, in addition to that cotton field situation pertaining to work. All the sports, at the school were in the town of West Point, Mississippi; only the best situation possible for rural boy. I was self-taught, coached baseball team with a few of the older young men. We would practice only when it rained of doing the time that in summer, July and August, during the period, the cotton no longer needed someone to continue to cut the weeds, from around the cotton plants that would bear the cotton bowls. I would be allowed to participate in any type of sports activities, continue demanding in cultivation of the cotton crops...

Going back to Chicago, was my breakthrough for opportunities in education at all levels, including sports activities. Sports would become my passion, save my life, gave opportunities out of this world.

CHAPTER 18

MY IMAGINATION IS GOING WILD

I know that that little Charles in me would come out an persevere in any way possible. He has always been there when I need him to help me – I call that the "God" in me.

My living quarter would always appear to be something that was second compared to the friends that I was attracted to (me as well, as they're attracted to me).

Parker High School was one of the best experiences any child would like to encounter. While attending parker high I enjoyed wrestling, track field, music, football. I had a varsity sweater, that carried all my letter, with which the activities I participated. After arriving to Chicago, summer I give almost all my money to my Step mother, the understanding that when school start, she would purchase my school supplies.

High at Parker High School, at 68th South Stewart in Chicago Illinois. This was the High School, I attended which change my life and restructured my future. The school allowed to dream of many possibilities and achievements. This was the transformation of the sharecropper grandson, to a real Chicagoan young man. While at the Junior High School, called Yale Upper Grade Center, I had also met friends, that lived east of the Dan Ryan highway in Chicago, the Interstate, that run in the middle of the Southside of Chicago; Little did I know, that most of Chicago gangs, were territorial, you couldn't go in areas without someone with you, like an adult (especially while in high school). The children's over the East side of the Dan Ryan most were middle class black's people. Some carried themselves just a little different than the people that lived on 70th and Normal Ave, one block south of Stewart where my high school was locate

High school, was a joyful time for me, learning pertaining, to new changes taking place in my life. Making that transition, from rural American to metropolitan American, making a transition of being extremely different. without currency, (money)which had haunted all of my childhood life, living on that plantation, my grandparents. Especially with me being so embarrassed continuously, I got older knowing my financial status, I stood compared to all my friends. I was associated with in the rural, West Point, Mississippi, Clay, County. That little boy that went to West Point Mississippi, that was confused pertaining to everything that was happening around him. Today, a little boy, was so confident that was sure of himself while living in Chicago. My mother, even as she struggled, so hard to make end's met, to make it possible to support five children, without adequate financial support.

That little Charles, would never stop believing, that he would get the best out of life regardless what he faced. God, just love saying to me just don't worry, everything is going to be all right. Just don't stop believing in what this inner spirit, continue to instruct you. This is what, keep me going all the time, while I lived on that Mr. James Thomas Brand Plantation. This is what keep me going, when I couldn't understand why I'm living with my grandparents, this what I felt, when I didn't have the proper clothes or shoes to compete visually in the eye of an onlooker. Most people, did judge you on what material things, that you would verify, you been a middle-class African American. In my opinion, if you have certain item, you are not hunger to receive those items. (Example; if you're not hungry you don't have the hunger to eat.) Once you have obtained certain status in life, the only objective necessary, for you to continue, is to do what you maintain, what you have. The value of having something, is knowing the value of the importance of keep the maintenance of it. (Example: its call the upkeep). What some sharecroppers, know was the value of maintenance, of those cotton crops in the cotton field, the generation prior to them. They didn't know the value maintain, a sacrificing their children getting an education, through any means necessary, in a positive manner. In my opinion my grandpa most had train me, to have some, his in the characteristics that he had, by being a sharecropper worker.

After returning to Chicago, I just looking at the advantage of opportunities. I wasn't sure of the direction, I would travel. One thing for sure, I wasn't going to pass up any situation, would allow me, to be a better person in my future. While in the rural part of West Point, in Clay, County, Mississippi. I had start picking up some of the characteristic, which that environment offered as a way of life. Oh yes! I had something to compare my newfound environment, Chicago. I first compared Chicago, with the city people of West Point, Miss. My eyes haven't traveled much further than the city life of the African American, at that time, I digested all I could, see that Chicago, had to offer there, were very few things to compare. However, I knew that hard work would put money in my pocket, create a good plan to earn for myself. I knew what I had to do. I didn't want to become some of those adults, that had left the rural, came back to visit without making progress, in their ways of life. I'm talking about the city West Point, MS., as well as the rural people.

Once again, the only dilemma, I face with, truly was the lodging in which that four-room apartment. We had at one time was seven people living in a four-room apartment in Chicago, that was poor standards, by comparison to other people, at that time, in that area. What an embarrassment to invited, a friend to my home, seeing like we lived in Chicago. I would override that living standard. I override my past in rural West Point, Mississippi, while living with my grandparents, as sharecroppers. I always said, to myself I'm better than this, encourage to better my own pride.

CHAPTER 19

BACK TO CHICAGO SCHOOL, REVIEW

My sister Ella, had moved by with our mother and stepfather in Chicago.
In the late 1950's

Ella, had become very elegance as rich articular, in her speaking, like a Chicagoan Dialect. She would use comforting words like generous person, in the place of freehearted person, which was on the Muda. During my first month, returning back to Chicago, being away in Rural West Point Mississippi, my world had just been upgraded to unlimited opportunities. From the moment I awakening to a full day of endless opportunities, to get Educated to catch up on so many educations fundamental, I hadn't received while living Rural West Point Mississippi.

RETURN BACK TO CHICAGO REVIEW

Everything were, as I had dreamed Chicago, would be. The people look as if I had traveled to a foreign country. My dreams, had not prepared me for so many changes that were occurring instantly. As we hit the city limit, of the inner City of Chicago, the traffic remained the same speed, some people that were driving had no regards for the speed limits. My father had no problem in keep up with the speed with the other vehicles.

I'm now in the Big City of Chicago. As we entered deeper and deeper into the City, on the South Side, where we would be living. My curiosity, just went out of control, just thinking about the apartment or house that we would be living in Chicago upon our arrival. To my disappointment, it's only a small made only for two or three, people at the most. My father had not made any adjustment, to take my brothers and I, into his home.

HIGH SCHOOL IN CHICAGO REVIEW

My High School, I attended was Parker High, School, located right down from Chicago Teachers College. Where the campus, were well kept. This campus were four times the size of Mary Holmes campus in West, Point, Mississippi. Someone would see my world changing over night with just a 720-mile trip from Mississippi, now in Chicago. This trip was a transformation every day. I couldn't make that trip, as a young boy living on James Thomas Brand, James, Quarter that was called, The Muda.

Little didn't I know of the day-to-day challenges, living with my stepmother and father that I hadn't lived with. What a life now I'm faced with.

My father, had dropped my brothers and me off, hadn't returned for us, to visit Chicago from Mississippi. Now, I'm in a situation, I'm in competition, the Chicago Boys, for a place in the community. How would I, fit in this community, large where people didn't speak to you, react to any of your concern pertaining to anything.

MISSISSIPPI LAWS REVIEW

The Mississippi laws, had implemented that any children's from out of state in Mississippi, couldn't attend school unless, adopted by the people in which the residents, of the people in which they were housed.

That was the reason, why we had to return back to Chicago. The Schools, were overflooded from children, coming with family, from the north, to live with family in Mississippi. The law, was based on preventing farmers, from having any benefits or advancements, in my opinion. There were no laws set aside to give the plantation worker any benefits pertaining to loss of wages or injuries while working on the farm during that time. If you were not physically or mentally able to work, you would not be compensated for time, lost from not working.

Upon my arrival to the Junior High School, there was a rapid acceleration course to be a city boy transformation, from a rural barefooted dress up on Sunday, country boy. Every day was, Sunday upon my arrival to Chicago and attending school.

Attending my High School, returning from Rural West point, Mississippi.

This was the most positive culture shock, from my point of view, as a High School freshman, in High School, anyone could have dream, would take place in their life. Upon my first days in High School in Chicago. I walked to the school building, as if I was in a capsule. I could see my environment around me, the positivity and negativities.

Returning to Chicago School

That children displayed now, in Rural Clay County, there were a similar reflection, I encountered in Rural School, nothing could compare the level, I now faced in a multitude, of confusion competition. Disarray that was continuous, once School was over, children didn't have anything to do once, School, was over for those day, children were out of School.

ARRIVAL TO MISSISSIPPI REVIEW

I found out that people children, did not work in fields; there were a great deal of leisure activities children participated in around the block. Children with nothing to do, you not working they created their own activities; where I lived activities were limited. Little did I know the activity is generally in the school, with the park district. School didn't have corporal punishment in the school system. In West Point, Mississippi, Clay County, the corporal punishment was very strong alive. Leisure time on the Chicago Southside Streets, appears the great deal of people appear to have the street hustling would be visible.

Around Chicago, my amazing of observation, were filled wall-to-wall buildings everywhere, once again concrete everywhere possible now! The rules of supervision, became a major objective for the children in Chicago, the rules for almost everything possible. Rules, were in place for every situation, including time to be children had to report their home, at a particular age group, your parents were accountable for the children's, behavior or misconduct with consequences. I observed, more than everything the street. Where people taking advantage of people, didn't have knowledge pertaining to a situation. There were people, cared about people certain situation, kind peoples in those after School Programs. How can I fit in this environment? I have come from the Cotton Field off of a Plantation, where hard work was a part of it all even just thinking about my past and rural West Point Mississippi. While in the rural West Point, Mississippi, most of my friends, were middle class and a blue-collar worker that had their own property. I live daily that someday they would find out how poor my grandparents, were, that I lived on that plantation.

From my observation, I saw the children in Junior High and High School, taking from students that were, innocent to the fact that those children, their kind hearts every opportunity possible. My friends associated me, in West Point, Mississippi, with my aunt Connie and uncle Perl; living as middle class, African American, we were respected by the community by all standards.

In some situations, some of the children, were afraid of some other children. just known as bully students, the beginning of gangs. Members, that took a different view about what was fair, Street smart students, could have their way with those students that hadn't been in that environment. Taking their lunch money, almost robbing them in some situation, students with hard lives, taking from those that have no recourse, getting relief from reporting them to the teachers, were in charge of the classes. Strong people, take advantage of kindness as a weakness.

In West Point Mississippi, rural clay county, working in those Cotton Fields, manual labor cutting firewood, hauling hay, shopping cotton, and picking cotton, eating good fashion rural food home grown, develops my physical body, protected me from those bullies at the school.

In the neighborhood, my display my boxing skills. Yes, back in Chicago one leisure time activities for children was Street boxing, consisted of only as punching, on the body, including arms never head in the face under any circumstance. Street boxing, was the same as boxing, there weren't any referees to call foul. Now that God, whom I had prayed to during that time in Clay County, had start growing, in me with his leadership, excellent common sense, making any adjustments that I face daily without any difficulties. Regardless of what the situation may surface. I had excellent physical genetics, from my very physically strong father, along with my physically strong mother brothers.

Once again, that mourner bench, God, I had been acquainted with while during my praying, desperation of hope as well as survivor. while living in Rural Clay, County, God re-surface to come to my rescue in my dreams, gave me a vision of what I need to do.

My father had a beautiful strong body, he worked physically in construction. My father had a massive body strength. My mother's brother also displays a beautiful physical physique, while coming up the rates at Bryan Packing Company, worked on the killing floor, they had to execute the cattle as well as hogs for processing. Uncle Perl wife aunt Connie was my aunts only by marriage, she treated me, as if I was her son. Aunt Connie and uncle Perl, was a strong man in West Point, Mississippi, physically around the entire town. Once the town yearly livestock fair, his strength by ring the bell, for a teddy bear, with only one hand at the carnival fair. By taking of one of those sludge hammers, to ring the bell by hammering the red dot to the top of the scale. This measure excellent in order to receive a prize, that accomplishment. I would just stand back, just look at the enjoyment, he had while making that accomplishment, winning ladies, teddy bears from that activity. Yes, he was indeed very excellent entertainer.

This is what provided, me from being taken advantage of physically. I was not ready for the things my stepmother, as a child of 15 years of age. Ida, was very unpredictable always. Ida, was a lady that, just when, I thought we were getting along, something would happen to start this mental confusing behavior that she displayed. Ida, was a person who drink daily and sometime she would drink socially as well as drink alone. She was not always compassion for me, once again her eyes shine as she looked at me as her older son. She never able to compensate for the last time, while living with my grandparents, my eyes always asked me to please forgive her for that time. My mother knew, I was more of a Johnson, in her heart then a Watkins. My mother her mother Ella, while visiting her in rural Prairie County, Mississippi, mama Ella, all grandchildren called her tell me, that I look more and more like her boys, uncle Perl, Cal, and Sam. Now upon my arrival, I begin to feel, act in the way they carried themselves, all three of them had worked their way to the top of their jobs positions as top managers. Perl and Cal with Bryan Packing Company. Sam, was a driving trainer instructor, with the Chicago Transit Authority.

Once I cleaned myself up, I feel as if, I was as good as anyone around. Regardless, of their financial status, what race they may be. Once, I found, the things to do to get ahead immediately, I start doing them, I needed money, I got me a little weekend job washing dishes, in a restaurant on Pulaski Street. Little did I know, this foundation, I had established was preparing me to become an athlete. I could display my argue, my frustration on the wrestling team, football field, track and field, and singing in the all-boys chorus (with a tremendous chorus instructor that didn't tolerate nothing but the best).

While in High School, I selected having chorus sing over physical education class. Yes! These were the choice, I made prevent me from making more mistake.

MY GRANDFATHER POEM

My grandfather was Charles Watkins Sr., a sharecropper;
his father was a slave.
My grandfather's father was named Charlie Watkins.
I think they might have upgraded my grandfather name to Charles
Watkins.

It's was the Best thing to do with the new birth of Education.

Yes! My grandfather cultivated my life in same aspect – he cultivated my life in the area of being accountable.

Yes, my grandfather cultivated my life.

My grandfather allows me to grow in the highest areas, in which the community would allow a young negro boy to grow without feeling to uppity.

What would a poor plantation boy fit in a poor community without "threatening" people with authority within the society being seen as a "troublemaker".

My grandfather, has taking over my life.

I look to my grandfather for my grandmother support, she was limited to making money.

My grandmother could not get a job in which African American men totally controlled.

What equal right, what equal pay, what equal equality, not shared openly around the sharecropper working men.

PAINTINGS BY CHARLES WATKINS III

Pullman Porters

Precious Time

African American Gothic detail

Sharecroppers Daughter

Daughter with pride dogs

Welcome Home

Sharecroppers daughter II

Westerner

Three Sharecropper Daughters

For the Love

Movements of the Sharecroppers Daughter

Self Portrait

© Charles Watkins III

BIBLIOGRAPHY

1.) https://en.wikipedia.org/

2.) Frank Lawrence Owley. "King Cotton Diplomacy: Foreign Relation of the Confederate States of America" Tuscaloosa: University of Alabama Press, c. 1931.

3.) David Christy. "Cotton is King: or the Culture of Cotton and its Relation to Agriculture, Manufactures, and Commerce" Derby & Jackson, New York; H. W. Derby & Co., Cincinnati, c. 1856 https://books.google.com/books?id=JnlXAAAAYAAJ&pg=PP1

4.) Tennessee Ernie Ford, Merle Travis (lyricist). "Sixteen Tons" Capitol Records, 1947.
https://www.youtube.com/watch?v=jIfu2A0ezq0 - Performed by Ernie Ford
https://www.youtube.com/watch?v=5pfVvqLM_e4 - Performed by Merle Travis

5.) Wikipedia. "Sixteen Tons" https://en.wikipedia.org/wiki/Sixteen_Tons

6.) Biography.com Editors. "William Tecumseh Sherman" *A&E Television Networks* http://www.biography.com/people/william-tecumseh-sherman-9482051

7.) Henry Louis Gates Jr. "Many Rivers To Cross: The Truth Behind '40 Acres and a Mule'"
http://www.pbs.org/wnet/african-americans-many-rivers-to-cross/history/the-truth-behind-40-acres-and-a-mule/

8.) Kenneth E. Philips. "Sharecropping and Tenant Farming in Alabama" July 28th, 2008
http://www.encyclopediaofalabama.org/article/h-1613

9.) Wikipedia. "Sharecropping" https://en.wikipedia.org/wiki/Sharecropping

10.) National Cotton Council of America. "The Story of Cotton: History of Cotton" Cordova, Tennesee. https://www.cotton.org/pubs/cottoncounts/story/

11.) Board of Governors of the United States Federal Reserve System, "May 1923,"
Federal Reserve Bulletin. Federal Reserve Board, 1914-1935. May, 1923. *Pg.* 567 https://fraser.stlouisfed.org/scribd/?item_id=20548&filepath=/files/docs/publications/FRB/1920s/frb_051923.pdf

12.) Thomas Weiss, "U.S. Labor Force Estimates and Economic Growth, 1800-1860",
American Economic Growth and Standards of Living before the Civil War;
University of Chicago Press, January 1992. *pg.*19 – 78
http://www.nber.org/chapters/c8007.pdf http://papers.nber.org/books/gall92-1

13.) Cotton's Journey Website, "Story of Cotton", *Cotton's Journey Curriculum*, Hanford, CA.
http://www.cottonsjourney.com/storyofcotton/page3.asp
Cotton's Journey is an independent organization that offers a curriculum and academic resources centered around the importance of cotton in history and in life to elementary and high schools. More information: http://www.cottonsjourney.com/Contactinfo/default.asp

14.) Cotton Incorporated, "Cotton Market Fundamentals & Price Outlook", *Monthly Economic Letter*, April 2017.
http://www.cottoninc.com/corporate/Market-Data/MonthlyEconomicLetter/

15.) K. Raja Reddy[1], H. F. Hodges[1], J. J. Read[2], J. M. Mckinion[2], J. T. Baker[3], L. Tarpley[4] And V. R. R Eddy[3], "Soil-Plant-Atmosphere-Research (SPAR) Facility: A Tool For Plant Research And Modeling" [1]*Department of Plant and Soil Sciences, Mississippi*

State University, [2]USDA-ARS, Genetics and Precision Agriculture Research Unit Mississippi State University, [3]USDA-ARS, Remote Sensing and Modeling Laboratory, BARC-West, Maryland, [4]Texas A &M Research and Extension Center, Beaumont, Texas.
Vol. 30, July 20th, 2001. http://www.spar.msstate.edu/class/EPP-2008/Chapter%201/Reading%20material/Facilities/SPAR_Biotronics.pdf

16.) The National Cotton Council of America, "Boll Weevil Eradication: A Complete Success," http://www.cotton.org/tech/pest/bollweevil/eradication2.cfm

17.) Frederick J. Perlak. "Development And Commercial Use Of Bollgard Cotton In The USA--Early Promises Versus Today's Reality". Plant Journal. 27(6):489-501, September 2001 https://www.ncbi.nlm.nih.gov/pubmed/11576434

18.) http://bermudagrass.com

19.) Wikipedia.org, "Samuel Slater" https://en.wikipedia.org/wiki/Samuel_Slater

20.) Wikipedia.org, "Cotton Gin" https://en.wikipedia.org/wiki/Cotton_gin

21.) **BLOG** by Janice Person. "Cotton 101: Can you eat cotton or cottonseed?"
February 28th, 2012. http://janiceperson.com/cotton/cotton-101-eat-cotton-cottonseed/

22.) National Cotton Council of America. "Cotton", *Robinson Library*. Updated April 2017.
http://www.robinsonlibrary.com/agriculture/plant/field/cotton.htm

23.) Wikipedia.org. "Gossypol" https://en.wikipedia.org/wiki/Gossypol

24.) Texas FFA Association. "Farm Facts", *2016 Senior FFA Quiz*, 2016-17 Officer Candidate Testing Program, pg. 26. https://www.texasffa.org/docs/FINAL%202016-17%20Texas%20Farm%20Facts_34932.pdf

25.) **FORUM POST** by Ed Wrather, "Cotton Chopping", *InspirationalArchive.com,*
http://www.inspirationalarchive.com/863/cotton-chopping/

26.) B. Touchstone Hardaway. "Walking Plows: Plowing with Horses, Mules and Oxen" *MotherEarthNews.com,* April, 1978. http://www.motherearthnews.com/homesteading-and-livestock/walking-plows-zmaz74zhol

27.) "Amish farming with antique plow and Belgian horses" November 16th, 2013. https://www.youtube.com/watch?v=UWOgXzqzcj0

28.) [1]Gary Martin, [2]Dave Wilton. "Cotton-Picker", "Cotton-Picking" [1]http://www.phrases.org.uk/meanings/cotton-picking.html [2]http://www.wordorigins.org/index.php/cotton_picking/

29.) Smithsonian, "International Harvester Mechanical Cotton Picking Machine", *National Museum of American History, Kenneth E. Behring Center.* http://americanhistory.si.edu/collections/search/object/nmah_857080

30.) Bill Ganzel, "Cotton Harvesting", *LivingHistoryFarm*.org. The Ganzel Group. c. 2007.
http://www.livinghistoryfarm.org/farminginthe50s/machines_15.html

31.) Donald Holley (University of Arkansas Monticello). "John Daniel Rust", *Encyclopedia of Arkansas' History and Culture*, June 2003. http://www.encyclopediaofarkansas.net/encyclopedia/entry-detail.aspx?entryID=2272

32.) Holley, Donald (University of Arkansas Monticello). "Mechanical Cotton Picker".
EH.Net Encyclopedia, edited by Robert Whaples. June 16, 2003. http://eh.net/encyclopedia/mechanical-cotton-picker/